Troubled Children and Youth

Turning Problems into Opportunities

Larry Brendtro
Mary Shahbazian

Research Press 2612 N Mattis Avenue Champaign, Illinois 61822
(800) 519-2707 www.researchpress.com

5   4   3   2   1   03   04   05   06   07

Composition by Jeff Helgesen
Cover design by Linda Brown, Positive I.D. Graphic Design, Inc.
Printed by Malloy, Inc.

ISBN 0-87822-489-0
Library of Congress Control Number 2003108545

This book is dedicated to the memory of our colleague Dr. Arnold P. Goldstein (1934–2002), a pioneer in searching for strength-based solutions with challenging youth. For over two decades, he directed the Center for the Study of Aggression at Syracuse University. At the time of his death, Dr. Goldstein was a nominee for the Nobel Peace Prize. He also was to receive the Spirit of Crazy Horse Award at the Black Hills Seminars on Reclaiming Youth: The honor was given posthumously and accepted by his wife, Susan. One of the most cited authors in this field, he left a legacy including 80 books and 100 articles.

Contents

Acknowledgments

Troubled Children and Youth: Turning Problems into Opportunities is a collaboration between Reclaiming Youth, a nonprofit research and training institute, and the Allendale Association, an organization that has served children and families from the Chicago area for more than a century. Research for this project was supported by grants from the W. K. Kellogg Foundation; Augustana College in Sioux Falls, South Dakota; and the Allendale Shelter Club. This model of strength-based intervention was piloted in educational, treatment, and juvenile justice settings by the Life Space Crisis Intervention Institute, Hagerstown, Maryland; Charlevoix-Emmet Intermediate School District, Charlevoix, Michigan; Starr Commonwealth Schools, Albion, Michigan; Youth Off The Streets, Sydney, Australia; and the Allendale Association, Lake Villa, Illinois. The authors are especially grateful to the youth and families who shared their stories of struggle and survival.

Introduction

Children present their own unique private logic about the world, which is often a mystery to adults. This is particularly true with youngsters who display emotional and behavioral problems. This book offers a fresh perspective on the challenges presented by these youths in their families, schools, and communities.

Troubled Children and Youth blends research-validated strategies for strength-based treatment with the positive philosophy of early youth work pioneers. This project was commissioned by the Allendale Association, which began serving wayward boys from the streets of Chicago in the late 19th century. Over the years, Allendale has developed educational and treatment programs that have helped thousands of troubled girls and boys find new hope for their lives.

Allendale was founded in 1894 by Captain Edward Bradley and his wife, Maud Bradley. They began with $25 and a group of six cast-off kids from Chicago's Home for the Friendless. They set up a temporary camp on the shores of a lake north of the city. From the beginning, "misfit and unwanted children" were always welcome, and the ethos was never to give up on a difficult child. The Bradleys believed children were self-corrective and would outgrow problems in the right environment. Problems were evidence not of depravity of youth, but of disrupted relationships and "poisonous environments." The Bradleys established Allendale "not so much to ameliorate certain false conditions as upon a deep and abiding faith in boykind" (Bradley & Bradley, 1926, p. 22).

An early Associated Press article painted Allendale youth in less than stellar terms. The Bradleys were outraged that anybody dared describe their kids as bad: "We believe that Allendale boys are the very best boys in the world. That is how family pride feels and thinks. . . . [W]e put forward no claims that we 'make good boys' because we have discovered that they are generally already made" (p. 54).

Despite the best of intentions, there sometimes was a mismatch between a particular youth and adult. In the event of continual negative reports from a staff member, the usual solution was to "transfer the malefactor" to another group, where the youngster might have a better chance for success. One youngster remarked, "Seems to me our cottage is getting all the scrapings from other cottages. Anyway, they don't *stay* scrapings" (p. 57).

The ethos of Allendale was to cultivate strengths rather than punish deviance. Allendale students participated in the governance of their "junior municipality" and were taught to take responsibility for one another. Each Thanksgiving, children raised money to benefit those even less fortunate. By caring for others, young people came to discover their own worth and competence.

A century ago, the Bradleys fought against punitive treatment, which left troubled children "sunk in a swamp of social resentment, tangled up in a coil of punishments from which there seems no escape" (p. 55). They put their faith in young people others saw as hopeless. In that spirit, we invite the reader to recast problems of today's youth as opportunities instead of threats. Part I explores challenges presented by troubled and troubling children. Part II highlights practical and proven solutions for addressing these problems.

Many people affect the lives of youth—parents, educators, helping professionals, policy leaders, and mentors. All seek to make sense of the behavior presented by children. *Troubled Children and Youth* resonates with the hope that every young person might find some grown-up who understands.

PART I
Challenges

CHAPTER ONE
Crisis and Courage

The history of childhood in Western civilization chronicles centuries of cruelty and neglect. Children had the legal status of chattel—like slaves, livestock, and other property. If they caused trouble, they were severely punished or abandoned. At a tender age, many were sold into servitude, breaking all family bonds. Victims of this abuse grew up to become the next generation of abusive adults (de Mause, 1974). With their most basic needs denied, these children displayed all manner of disturbed behavior, and adults responded with harsh punishment. Nine-year-old Mary Woton was such a child. She was hauled before a London court in 1735 by the family to whom she had been apprenticed. The court records read: "Mary Woton was indicted for stealing twenty-seven guineas and a half, and four Shillings and six Pence, the money of Mr. John Easton. . . . The Jury found her guilty. She was sentenced to death" (Sanders, 1970, p. 34).

Approaches to discipline are shaped by the "folk psychology" of a culture (Rogoff & Morelli, 1989). Because predemocratic Western civilization was organized around dominance and subjugation, education and child rearing fit this mold. With the advent of democratic ideals in Europe, leaders in youth work broke sharply with these totalitarian practices. They believed that all children had potential and should be treated with dignity. Problem behavior was seen as evidence of discouragement. With this diagnosis, they sought to build hope and courage in even the most challenging children.

COURAGE BUILDERS

What we want to achieve in our work with young people is to find and strengthen the positive and healthy elements, no matter how deeply they are hidden.

—Karl Wilker (1920, p. 69)

The optimistic philosophy of early youth professionals sprang from the pioneering work of Swiss educational reformer Johann Pestalozzi (1746–1827). Pestalozzi founded orphanages and schools for urchins who roamed the streets of European cities after the Napoleonic wars. He described his cast-off kids as arrogant and ignorant, filthy and vermin-covered. Yet he was convinced that beneath these faults were precious qualities waiting to be discovered.

In the 19th century, Dorothea Dix (1802–1887) became the most prominent advocate for the positive treatment of emotionally troubled people. She began her work teaching Sunday school for imprisoned girls and young women. Outraged at the conditions she saw, Dix set out to expose abusive practices such as locking children in jails and stables. Her personal campaign sparked a worldwide mental health movement. She called for the creation of environments where a "spirit of excellence" permeated all activities in the hope that "the young mind through these may be won to truth and virtue" (Dix, 1845, p. 93).

In this same era, an idealistic group of young medical doctors founded what later became the American Psychiatric Association. They created highly successful healing communities that virtually eliminated harsh punishments and locked isolation.[1] Historians described their methods as based on the development of close helping relationships: "The physicians spare no effort in gaining the confidence and good will of their patients and strive to discover their experiences and supply their needs" (Bockhoven, 1956, p. 175).

Jane Addams (1860–1935) was a leader in the movement to establish children's courts for abused and delinquent children. She also sought to unleash "the spirit of youth" by appealing to adventure, idealism, and social purpose. Schools and churches became community centers providing rich activities and responsive adults. Addams democratized helping professions so workers would convey respectful humility rather than blame the person in difficulty (Addams, 1909).

By the First World War, treatment for troubled children was becoming a recognized profession. Polish physician Janusz Korczak (1879–1942) worked with Jewish street children in Warsaw and brought new methods to juvenile courts. Korczak penned 20 books, with titles that included *How to Love a Child* and *The Child's Right to Respect.* With the Nazi occupation of Poland, Korczak and his staff and children were incarcerated in the Warsaw ghetto. In a final test of his alliance with children, Korczak rejected offers for safe passage and chose to climb onto the chlorinated boxcars and accompany his children to the gas chambers of Treblinka (Brendtro & Hinders, 1990).

Maria Montessori (1870–1952) created controversy by becoming Italy's first female physician, a position that required approval from the pope. As a young doctor, she set out to reclaim children from the slums of Rome. She was the first to describe the two basic types of problem children, those who act out in defiance of adults and those who retreat in despair. Whether children were "strong" or "weak," she developed methods to engage these reluctant students and tap the potential of their highly "absorbent minds" (Montessori, 1948).

Anton Makarenko (1888–1939), from the Ukraine, worked with street delinquents who terrorized Russian cities after the revolution. He created a rich program of productive activities designed to teach joy and develop positive "future perspectives." A teacher once approached Makarenko to complain that she had no hope in a particular youth. Makarenko told the teacher that she would no longer be allowed to have any contact with that young person (Makarenko, 1976).

Youth work pioneers espoused progressive approaches in an era when democracy was still a fragile flower. In Korczak's terms, the challenge was to treat all children with respect, recognizing that they are *citizens in embryo.* But these philosophies were far ahead of their time in political systems that were still highly authoritarian and punitive. European nations had mounted the pinnacle of materialism and military might, subduing simpler societies on every continent. But in this pursuit of power, Western culture had torn the family and tribal bonds that had sustained human communities since the dawn of civilization.

CIRCLES OF COURAGE

Throughout most of human history, the tribe or extended family shared the responsibility of rearing children. If biological parents were too young, were irresponsible, or died, children were nurtured by caring adults who passed on the values of the culture. Many tribal peoples believe that every child needs many mothers and fathers. This belief is typical of many aboriginal cultures in which children are treated with great dignity and respect. For example, the Lakota word for *child* means "sacred being." In the Maori language, a child is addressed as "gift of the gods." These values were threatened by the European drive to "civilize" so-called primitive peoples.

Colonial powers saw their destiny as dominating "primitive" cultures. Native children were torn from their families and placed in punitive boarding schools, where they were beaten to purge their traditional beliefs. Stripped of cultural connections, those of this "stolen generation," as they are called by contemporary aboriginal Australians, were unable to effectively rear their own young. European conquerors were unaware that most tribal peoples had sophisticated systems of rearing respectful, responsible children. Herbert Vilakazi of South Africa has called for reclaiming these lost truths, including the wisdom about child psychology that emerged from his African culture:

> I know of no people more concerned about child psychology, and very meticulous and systematic in their consideration of children, than pre-industrial peasants. . . . What we should do, in our efforts to increase and improve our knowledge of child psychology, is to study not only what child psychologists have written, but also the theory of childhood contained in peasant cultures, and to then integrate or synthesize the two. (1993, p. 37)

In North America, the native tribes developed strategies for rearing respectful children without using harsh punishment. These philosophies were refined over thousands of years in cultures where the central purpose of life was nurturing children. Psychological research is only now reaching the point where such approaches can be understood and replicated. This philosophy of child development has been called the Circle of Courage (Brendtro, Brokenleg, & Van Bockern, 1990, 2002) and is relevant to the challenges faced by contemporary youth.

Native American psychologist Martin Brokenleg and colleagues described the Circle of Courage model for creating environments in which all children can thrive (Brendtro, Brokenleg, & Van Bockern, 1990, 2002). This approach blends youth developmental research, the heritage of youth work pioneers, and Native American philosophies of child care. Lakota artist George Blue Bird portrayed the Circle of Courage in the medicine wheel in Figure 1.1 on page 8.

All children need opportunities to experience belonging, mastery, independence, and generosity. The Circle of Courage shifts the focus from controlling problems to developing strengths. Youth work pioneers since Pestalozzi advocated similar ideas as they struggled to reform cultures that did not respect children. The power of Circle of Courage principles lies in their simplicity. They reflect universal truths about valuing children and are validated by an emerging science of positive youth development. We briefly examine each principle in turn.

Belonging

With opportunity for attachment, a child learns, "I can trust." In traditional tribal groups, the entire community revered children. Lakota anthropologist Ella Deloria described the core value of belonging in Native American culture in these simple words: "Be related, somehow, to everyone you know" (Deloria, 1943, as cited in Brendtro, Brokenleg, & Van Bockern, 1990, 2002). Treating others as kin forged powerful social bonds that drew all into relationships of respect. Theologian Martin Marty observed that throughout history, the tribe, not the nuclear family, ensured the survival of the culture. Although parents

Figure 1.1

Circle of Courage

Generosity

Belonging

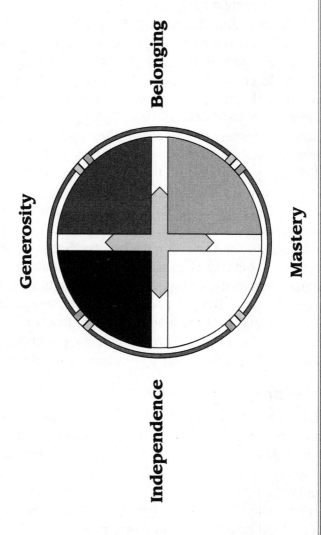

Independence

Mastery

8

might falter, the tribe was always there to nourish and guide the next generation.

Mastery

With opportunity for achievement, a child learns, "I have talent." The first lesson in traditional Native American culture was to carefully observe those with more experience in order to learn from them. The child was taught to see someone with greater skill or wisdom as an esteemed model for learning, not as a rival. Youth were encouraged to strive for mastery for personal attainment rather than to prove superiority over others. A person who became the best must not display arrogance but be willing to help others acquire this ability.

Independence

With opportunity for autonomy, a child learns, "I have power." The only way to distribute power to all is to respect each person's independence, a central principle of democracy. Education was designed to teach inner discipline and respect for all people and all life. From the early days of childhood, children were encouraged to make decisions, solve problems, and grow in responsibility. Adults modeled, nurtured, taught values, and gave feedback. Children were given abundant opportunity to make choices without coercion.

Generosity

With opportunity for altruism, a child learns, "My life has purpose." The principal virtue in Native American culture was generosity. This involved not only sharing physical resources, but giving time, showing respect, and practicing a forgiving nature. From early childhood, children were taught generosity. For example, at wakes and funerals, children had the honor of waiting on elders who were grieving. Children were told in many ways, "Whenever you get something good, give it away and see how far the good can spread."

The Circle of Courage applies across cultures and the life span because it is rooted in universal human needs. Belonging, mastery, independence, and generosity are essential to healthy development. In a normal progression, a child attaches to caring adults who help the child achieve, gain autonomy, and contribute to others. Thus the Circle of Courage provides a blueprint for creating environments in which all children can thrive and develop resilience.

An example of a resilient youngster is Tommy, a tossed-about teen who has spent his life in the foster care system. He was abandoned in a Dumpster immediately after his mother left the hospital where she gave birth to him. After years of being shuttled between foster homes, Tommy became the poster boy in a Midwest adoption promotion. A hundred families inquired about this handsome boy with the heart-wrenching story. Deplorably, the chosen adoptive family sexually abused him. Tommy is now in a residential treatment program that employs the Circle of Courage philosophy. He is not discouraged and still has hope for a real home. In his words, "I know I'm getting older but maybe one of the other 99 families still wants me." One of his counselors recently related how Tommy explained the Circle of Courage to a newcomer: "This is the plan for making your life whole."

DISCONNECTED CHILDREN

What counts most in life? . . . We need to connect—or reconnect—to our friends, our families, our neighbors, our communities.

—Edward M. Hallowell (1999, p. xi)

To thrive, children need social communities that nurture their physical, emotional, intellectual, and spiritual needs. According to psychologist Urie Bronfenbrenner, absolute minimum dosage of connection for each child is at least one adult who is irrationally crazy about him or her. Many children are deprived of even this slim diet of human nurturance (Bronfenbrenner, 1986). Psychiatrist Edward Hallowell contends that most symptoms of troubled behavior signal a deficiency in human connections.

"All I want is some kind of noticement!" wrote a youngster in a message to a teacher. Modern society is producing a host of disconnected, discouraged children. Living in emotional and spiritual crisis, they ponder the most basic existential questions: "Why was I even born?" "Who would even miss me if I died?" Without bonds to adults, children do not internalize prosocial values. Disrupted connections are pervasive in the contemporary family, school, peer group, and community (Hallowell, 1999).

Families on the Edge

We were discussing parenting in traditional cultures with a youth worker from a small Polynesian island. She said that, because all children have many parenting adults, in her tribal language there is no specific word for "mother" or "father." Instead, these terms translate as "male caregiver" and "female caregiver." By this standard, the modern nuclear family is seriously shorthanded. Even in relatively stable families, there is an erosion in the quantity of time that hurried and stressed parents can spend in genuine interaction with children.

Research has identified hundreds of factors that heighten family tension. Some stressors come from the broader culture, such as racism, poverty, and media violence. Many pressures relate to the isolated nuclear family, such as lack of proximity to relatives, divorce, single parenting, and limited child care options. The most immediate stressors are unique to the environment of a particular family. Examples include harried work schedules, financial problems, poor housing, illness, substance abuse, and family conflict. Whatever the cause, severe and chronic stress in the family interferes with positive parenting and weakens the parent-child bond (Dishion, French, & Patterson, 1995).

Stressed parents often make faulty judgments about their child's behavior and motivations. Normal problems are misconstrued as intentional defiance, and trivial issues are magnified into major conflicts. Parents wrapped up in their own problems may not empathize with their children. They are prone to thinking errors such as blaming and assuming the worst. Overstressed, they abandon reason and affection and discipline with threats, punishment, and assertions of power.

Throughout most of human history, the family was secure and the external environment was dangerous. In modern society, children are shorn of relatives, surrounded by strangers, and subjected to risks they can neither understand nor manage. Faced with threat, children instinctively seek the safety of trusted adults. However, if caregivers are a source of danger, the child literally has nowhere to go for protection: "The family that should be safe is dangerous. The outside world which should be approached warily is safer than home. Children in this predicament may experience nothing as safe" (Glantz & Pearce, 1989, p. 78).

Children have the genetic potential to adapt resiliently to a variety of "good enough" environments (Winnicott, 1965). But this does not include violence and abuse. Nothing in the genetic code equips a child for a two-front war against a dangerous world and dangerous elders.

Family breakup and single parenting affect children in different ways. In some cases, divorce reduces conflict but produces other stressors, including economic instability and interruption of regular contact between parents and children. Some children from divorced families report social embarrassment, fantasies of parental reconciliation, and fears of being abandoned by both parents. Still, resilient coping is the most common outcome among children from single-parent and divorced families (Emery & Kitzmann, 1995).

Distrust in the family is far more devastating than divorce (Strommen, 1988). Children are particularly distressed by conflicts between parents (Stone, Buehler, & Barber, 2002). Even if parents try to suppress disagreement, hostility is likely to leak through. Unspoken resentments of parents can be displaced on children in angry attacks or subtly, in sarcasm, hostile teasing, and the silent treatment. When parents openly battle one another, children are in the crossfire. One parent may denigrate the other or recruit a child in an alliance against the spouse.

Poverty amplifies all risks. Still, the great majority of lower income parents are sensitive to their children's needs and invest deeply in caring for their children (Furstenberg, Cook, will be well adjusted depends less on the neighborhood than on what happens in the life space of home and school. In many neighborhoods, good parenting is more prevalent than good schools or social services.

Conflict in School

Bonds to school foster positive development. Supportive teachers who cultivate success are particularly critical for students who experience conflict at home or in the community. Even if these outside problems cannot be eliminated, school mastery is a powerful stimulant to favorable life outcomes.

Many school conflicts do not originate there. A yearlong study of students with emotional problems in a Washington, D.C., day school showed a massive incidence of crisis in their lives (Parese, 2001). Forty-three percent of the students were homeless during the year. Seventy-one percent reported severe family stress, such as fighting with parents, running away from home, and incarceration or death of a family member. Schools can also *create* crisis in the lives of youth. All the youth experienced school violence, saw police arrest fellow students, and were distraught over the violent death of a classmate. This research indicates that schools need to provide support to students in times of crisis.

Decades of research at the University of Michigan have established a strong link between school failure and subsequent delinquency and disturbance (Gold, 1978; Gold & Mann, 1984; Gold & Osgood, 1992). Among beset students who are already anxious and depressed, school failure intensifies their symptoms of emotional disturbance. More socially buoyant youth often respond to school failure by finding peers who applaud their disruptive and defiant behavior. Adopting a delinquent identity actually increases tested self-esteem! A twofold intervention can reverse these problems. First, students need uncommonly warm emotional support from teachers. Second, students need abundant opportunities for success. Regardless of what else is happening in their lives, competence in school is a major boost to mental health.

School climate has a profound effect on the behavior and motivation of students (Hyman & Snook, 2001). *Positive school climates* help students feel that they belong and are respected. Students view discipline as fair and helpful. These schools have very low levels of ridicule, put-downs, and verbal assaults. Bullying and intimidation, whether from peers or staff, are strongly discouraged. Students enjoy regular attendance despite academic rigors. Such schools can become islands of security and hope for children in crisis.

In *negative school climates*, educators view students and families as adversaries rather than people to be valued and encouraged. Students see the school as rule bound and discipline as inconsistent and unfair. They believe that most staff do not really care about them. Bullying, ridicule, name calling, and put-downs—by both peers and staff—are rampant. Detention and suspension are routine. In schools with negative school climates, student alienation is widespread.

Although schools continually evaluate children, young people are seldom asked to share their own constructive observations. We turned the tables and invited two groups of high school students, from New England and the Midwest, to grade their schools.[2] For grading standards, students were asked how their school experience measured up to the Circle of Courage principles of belonging, mastery, independence, and generosity. These were typical comments describing both positive and negative school climates:

1. Does your school foster belonging?

   "It makes me feel like I belong when a teacher calls me by my first name even when I am not in their class." (Michelle)

   "Some of the teachers think they are too cool to talk to us. When you meet them in the hall, they put their heads down and look at the floor." (Helen)

2. Does your school foster mastery?

   "In many of my classes, I have felt that teachers really care about what they are doing and want us to learn and be successful in life. This makes me feel like I have accomplished something." (Gretchen)

"Some of my teachers really don't care about students like me. All they are interested in are the talented ones." (Rusty)

3. Does your school foster independence?

"I have gained plenty of responsibility. We want to be treated like young adults, and therefore we are given many choices." (Kraig)

"All through school, kids are herded around like sheep and left with almost nothing to decide upon." (Travis)

4. Does your school foster generosity?

"I would have liked to tutor someone or been a peer counselor. I have no idea how to get involved with a peer group, and I feel I could have helped someone and benefited from it myself." (Sondra)

"People who come from a negative home life, school is all they can look forward to and count on. I try to be nice to people and talk to people no one else will. I try to make them feel good about themselves." (Lance)

According to the Children's Defense Fund (2001), nearly 17,000 students are suspended and another 3,000 drop out in a typical year. The use of suspension has gone through cycles following the political philosophy of the times. In 1928, H. H. Davis published data from the previous four decades. Suspension declined 80 percent during that period, and corporal punishment was banned from most schools. More recently, "zero tolerance" has become a political code word, justifying suspension. David Osher (2000) reports school suspension doubled in a period of two decades until more than three million students were being suspended annually. Often this is an overreaction to irritating but nonviolent offenses. Fully 70 percent of suspensions in Milwaukee, Wisconsin, were for refusal to follow instructions or do work, classroom disruption, and profanity. The philosophy of the school and principal drives suspension rates. In four similar Miami,

Florida, schools, suspension varied from almost none to nearly 40 percent. There are great racial disparities in suspension, and half of the male African American students in some schools are suspended (Kipnis, 1999).

Schools are among the safest places in our communities, but highly publicized violence causes widespread fear of violence. The U.S. Secret Service studied multiple shootings occurring over a period of 25 years (Vossekuil, Reddy, Fine, Borum, & Modzeleski, 2000). Most shooters had experienced bullying and persecution reaching the level of torment. Others were overwhelmed by life problems, including school suspension. Rarely was violence impulsive; these kids do not "just snap." Many attackers had created art or poetry with themes of homicide, suicide, and hopelessness. Most distressing, other kids usually knew of the impending trouble but did not share this with any adult.

School alienation is not limited to disadvantaged students. Psychologist Reed Larson (2000) equipped middle-class teens with pagers to track their activities and attitudes. Youth were randomly paged and asked to record their state of mind. At school, most students reported being bored more than a quarter of the time. Honor students and delinquents were bored more than half the time. Even if students were concentrating, they were likely to be motivated by grades, test scores, or fear of failure rather than interest. Larson concluded that the central task facing educators is to find "how to get the fires of adolescence lit."

Trouble with Peers

Positive peer bonds foster healthy growth. Psychiatrist Harry Stack Sullivan (1953) noted that the *chumships* among youth could help overcome problems from earlier, troubled relationships with adults. The cliques and chumships of elementary years broaden into "crowds" by adolescence. These groups provide youth with a ready-made "identity," complete with distinctive preferences in dress, music, and activities (Brown, 1990). Crowd labels shift with changing youth subcultures, but typical identities have included jocks, brains, loners, rogues, druggies, populars, and nerds. Close friends are usually drawn from within a crowd. Peer groups have far-reaching influences on values and behavior. They can provide a sense of love and belonging but also can mark members of other groups as outcasts (Hoover & Milner, 1998).

Although friendships can foster prosocial skills and values, they can also initiate youth into antisocial behavior. When operating in groups, youth often perform for their peers by joining in high-risk behaviors in defiance of adult norms. In his *Confessions,* St. Augustine describes how as a youth he plunged headlong into wild behavior with his companions as they tried to outdo one another, bragging about their wickedness.

At age one, children are highly self-centered, and half of peer-initiated contacts are negative. This drops to 3–6 percent in elementary school. But middle school shows an upturn in aggression. Among adolescent boys, merely being insulted, or dissed, can spark physical encounters. This bullying is related to a "brutality norm," in which aggression signifies manhood (Cairns & Cairns, 2000). Teen girls more typically hurt one another with social aggression, such as rumor spreading and group alienation.

Such problems are commonplace. In a typical year, 37 percent of high school students report having been in a physical fight, and 80 percent engage in bullying behavior such as teasing, threatening, or pushing others (Mulvey & Cauffman, 2001).

We were invited to consult in a school where bullying was rampant. A group of adolescent girls shunned by high-status students spent much of their free time in hostile exchanges. Each day, a different girl was the target of attack in a game of social survivor. When the principal brought them all together for a meeting, one girl screamed that somebody had just spray-painted the word *bitch* inside her locker. A second had just filed assault and harassment charges against several other girls. Already at the bottom of the pecking order, these outcast students were engaged in nonstop victimization of each other. Teachers and parents were either unaware of or unable to stop this peer tyranny.

Immediately after this explosive session with these girls, we met with the school's coaches. They came to discuss bullying problems encountered by male students on the school's athletic teams. The cross-country coach had just filed civil rights charges against the school, accusing football players of creating a hostile educational environment. In a male-bonding tradition of long duration, football players scapegoated those who chose less manly sports. Members of the cross-country team were called "faggots," and football players would "de-pants" them to see if "runners really have balls."

Children who distrust adults connect to peers with similar beliefs in order to feel comfortable and validated (McCord, 1990). They have a radar-like ability to search out other anti-authority peers. By fourth grade they begin hanging out with peers who support their views on aggression (Caspy & Moffitt, 1995; Farmer & Hollowell, 1994). Getting into trouble with peers is a common phenomenon, and teen crime is seldom a solo affair. For example, 90 percent of juveniles who commit robberies do so with friends (Mulvey & Cauffman, 2001). Antisocial behavior peaks in the teen years but drops off sharply as youth "grow out" of reckless youthful behavior. This movement toward responsibility comes from new social roles in the community as well as growth in emotional control with maturation. However, communities may offer youth little leeway for error, and youth are often excluded from positive bonds.

Loss of Community

Fritz Redl (1966) described the United States as an "underdeveloped country" in which citizens loudly profess their love of kids but practice neglect of children and hatred of youth. Youngsters who disrupt adults seldom have a support base. Whereas other special-needs children become targets of telethons, these children become the target of attack.

In *The Scapegoat Generation*, Michael Males (1996) documents how youth with problems are demonized to justify draconian punishment. For example, only the United States still allows children under 18 to be sent to prison for life or to be executed. Democracies worldwide have extended rights and protections to youth. The United States has moved in the opposite direction. A quarter of a century of Supreme Court decisions stripped many constitutional protections from youth, including freedom of speech, the right to redress grievances, freedom from unreasonable search and seizure, protection from cruel or unusual punishment, and even the basic right to gather in groups in public. Males also is critical of so-called liberal youth advocates who claim that teens need protection because they are young, dumb, and can't think rationally.[3]

Youthful problem behavior signals a lack of positive connections. Nationwide studies by the Search Institute identified 40 developmental assets that buttress positive youth development (Benson, 1997). These include internal strengths of the youth as well as external supports and positive expectations from families, schools, friends, faith communities, employers, and the community at large. Children lacking these assets present a host of difficulties, including substance abuse, risky sexual behavior, delinquency, school failure, and emotional problems. Many communities have used Search Institute surveys to inventory the developmental assets of their youth. At any economic level, a typical youth has less than half the assets needed to protect against risk. Eighty percent of the young people surveyed report that most adults in their community do not really care about youth.

Peter Benson (1997) calls for communities to reach out to "all kids as our kids." Otherwise, we are bankrupting our social capital. Schools that exclude students in the name of "zero tolerance" block their pathway to responsible citizenship. Insurance companies that "manage care" by withholding mental health treatment keep troubled youth from healing. Courts that warehouse youth to "protect the community" make government into an abusive parent. Landlords who follow "one strike and you're out" policies turn residents with problems into homeless families. Employers who refuse to hire youth with a history of substance use or delinquency condemn them to countercultures of outcasts. Faith communities that fail to embrace our prodigal sons and daughters cut them off from positive peers and spiritual roots.

The most fundamental conservative value is to protect and conserve the young. By this standard, discarding our most needy children is an act of violence. If a society really cared about its children, could there be any disposable kids?

"THE NIMBY KIDS"
Wanda's Story

Families of children with emotional and behavioral problems are often subject to a double bias: Whereas their children are demonized, parents are labeled as "dysfunctional" and "lousy parents." Emerging family support organizations such as the Federation of Families for Children's Mental Health enable parents to become powerful forces for change. Wanda Terry describes how she and other parents challenged blatant prejudice in her community.[4]

I received another call from my 11-year-old daughter's school about her behavior. This time she tried to wrestle a toy away from her teacher, who had taken it away from *her*. Charity has always carried a toy with her for security ever since she was raped when she was about three years old. She suffers from posttraumatic stress disorder (PTSD), depression, and oppositional defiant disorder. Her peers have been calling her names and making fun of her for years.

At the school, I was told they would call another Individualized Education Program (IEP) meeting and perhaps place my daughter at Mountainbrook, a day treatment center in Canton, Georgia. I felt defeated—they could not understand my daughter, and it seemed they were giving up on her. I was also told that Charity had been banging her head against the wall and floor during lunchtime. Charity told me that she knew she could not hit the kids for teasing her and calling her names, but it hurt so bad that it made her feel better to hurt herself.

My daughter's school had been big and brightly lit, with large windows and shiny floors. When we first visited Mountainbrook, we found a small, old brick building with interior concrete block walls and exposed bare pipes. A depressing feeling overwhelmed me, and I bit my lip to keep from crying. Surely this was a place where children were sent when no one wanted them or cared about them. No child deserved this sort of place. There was no gym, no library, no music room, no conference room, no art room, and only one toilet for the entire school, children and staff included.

By the time I met the counselor, I was in tears. She assured me that they would be moving soon to better facilities in Waleska, Georgia, a few miles north of the current location. It was an old structure but would be painted, and they would have much more space. Maybe my daughter would not have to stay at the bottom of the barrel for long.

The Mountainbrook staff all had special training and really did seem to care. Things went pretty well for about a month until I read in our local newspaper that Waleska City Council members had voted to oppose Mountainbrook's move. They were concerned about our "unruly students." Our children did have behavior problems, but I did not understand how they could affect the community. It was painful knowing that a town did not want them. Over and over, Gene Pitney's song "A Town without Pity" kept going through my mind. I felt as though a heavy weight had fallen on me.

About two weeks later, my husband, Dan, woke me earlier than usual and handed me the newspaper. I could tell by the expression on his face that it was bad news. Marguerite Cline, the current mayor of Waleska and former Cherokee County school superintendent, had written a commentary describing the Mountainbrook students in the most negative terms possible. It was suggested that they used vulgar language; were not loved, praised, bathed, or fed regularly; and they caused pain and grief to their parents. She wrote:

> My back yard does not need Mountainbrook and neither do many other back yards. Now when it comes to facilities like Mountainbrook, the acronym NIMBY is appropriate—Not In My Back Yard—and that is certainly the case in Waleska since residents have learned that this is being considered by the school board. (Cline, 1997, p. 4A)

I was crushed and my chest hurt. I called another mother whose child was at Mountainbrook. Wiping tears from my eyes, I read the article to her. Then anger took over. How dare this woman who did not know us or our children print these lies! We had to write the editor of the *Cherokee Tribune* and tell our side of the story. No way would we hide and keep silent. I knew we were going up against one of the "power" figures in the county, but I did not care. When it concerned my child, I would take up the challenge. The mayor had tried to seal our children's fate in the hellhole they were in, and I was not going to stand for it!

My daughter and her schoolmates deserved facilities equal to those that the so-called normal children had. Marguerite Cline and the school board were going to get the fight of their lives. We wrote letters to the paper arguing every point she had made. We contacted the news departments of all the local television stations, two of which came out to cover the story, meeting with my daughter and me. I wanted to show the public that our children were not monsters. We had to repair the damage that had been done to their image. On the second newscast, several parents and their children were also involved. Both news stories were supportive of us, and more parents wrote letters of support. Some of the older students at Mountainbrook even started calling themselves "the NIMBY kids."

We called school board members. Some were cold and cruel, others much nicer. A group of parents banded together. I cautioned them to be humble and beg for help since no one *had* to help us. Georgia's largest newspaper, the *Atlanta Journal-Constitution*, carried a front-page story in the local news section. We called various organizations to ask for letters of support and concern. We contacted members of the state board of education and special education departments, speaking with anyone who would listen. Students from Reinhardt College circulated a petition in favor of the move and volunteered to help. Because Mountainbrook had been located in a residential area, I went door-to-door to get the residents to sign a petition stating they had never lived in fear of our children and had never had any negative experiences with them. Everyone signed it.

Some days I felt as though I was not getting anywhere. Then I would get new leads on people to call, and I would be up and running again. When Alison was less able to help, Janice filled in. We encouraged the parents to have relatives and friends write to local papers to keep the issue fresh and in the news.

We started PTCA, a parent, teacher, and community advocacy group, which was the school's first support group. I was elected president, although I did not feel qualified. I started talking to the parents about showing pride about their children. We did not need to hide under the rocks. As Margie Dobbins, another parent, put it, "Our children aren't a problem in society but a part of it."

How is it that we have equal housing and equal employment opportunities but not equal schooling for children with mental and behavioral problems? Discrimination is still alive and well, but discrimination against the handicapped is illegal. To us, a lack of equal educational facilities was discrimination.

I feel good about myself and the work I have done, trying to relocate our school. Parents are now standing up proudly to be heard instead of hiding in shame. The mood of the staff at Mountainbrook seems more upbeat. We have control over our lives and our children's lives. I now realize that my purpose in life is to make a difference in these children's lives. I will not fail them. I am no longer angry with Marguerite Cline. She not only gave me a reason to go public, she spurred me with the strength and drive out of my anger to make changes for these children.

At the end of the school year, we had our annual awards and graduation program and celebrated with a covered-dish dinner. The crowd was three times larger than any before; some people had to stand in the hall during the program. Parents and community members signed up for the next PTCA meeting. This project continued over the summer. In October, after intervention by the U.S.

Office of Civil Rights, the Cherokee County Board of Education approved the Mountainbrook request to relocate our school to the Waleska community.

If you are one person and think you cannot go it alone, you are wrong. One person can make a difference. You have got to hang in there and not give up, even when sometimes it looks like it is all going downhill. Let people know that you will not give up, and that you are not going away.

NOTES

[1] These psychiatrists called their system "moral treatment," which meant not moralistic instruction but rather treating people with kindness and providing rich opportunities for learning and relationships. Most frontline workers were former teachers. Physicians also spent time in extensive direct conversations with patients. Twenty years of statistical reports showed very high success rates, with most mentally ill people returning to the community with improved functioning. As Karl Menninger (1963) notes, the flood of immigrants after the Civil War led to the return to large, depersonalized institutions that warehoused troubled adults and children. Optimism gave way to professional pessimism that mental illness was incurable.

[2] Adapted from Odney and Brendtro (1992). Reproduced with permission from *Journal of Emotional and Behavioral Problems*.

[3] Males made these remarks in an interview with youth editor Joan Braune (2002).

[4] Condensed from an article by Wanda Terry (1997) with permission of the journal *Reclaiming Children and Youth*.

CHAPTER TWO

Coping with Conflict

Anthropologist Margaret Mead studied youth who came of age amidst the social tranquility of Samoa. A remarkable feature of that culture was the ability of these islanders to prevent conflict. Comparing the traditions of the United States, she observed that "children who have been exposed to violence will need more help than others in learning to live and let live" (Mead, 1979, p. 235).

Whenever people interact, disagreement is inevitable. Conflict is a powerful force in human development for both good and ill (Shantz & Hartup, 1992). Although conflict is a normal reaction when any animal experiences threat, the human brain can redefine threat as any insult or act of disrespect. Deeply held beliefs in American culture legitimize violence as a solution to conflict. Nisbett and Cohen (1996) studied this "code of honor" among urban street youth and in the culture of white Southern males. In each group, any affront is likely to trigger sharp anger and a desire to strike back. They note that this macho "don't tread on me" ethos is deeply rooted in U.S. history. Alexander Hamilton, pictured on the $10 bill, was killed in a duel with Vice President Aaron Burr. A winner of two duels, President Andrew Jackson earned a place on the $20 bill.

Today's children are exposed to violence in the home, school, and community. Those displaying problems become targets of public hostility and often experience institutional abuse. As if this were not enough, by age 18 a child will have witnessed 16,000 simulated murders and 200,000 acts of violence on TV (Mitchell & McEldowney, 2002). Instead of learning to "live and let live," children learn to be "victim or victimizer." Aggressive beliefs and behaviors increase as children proceed through the elementary years (Aber, Brown, & Henrich, 1999). This chapter addresses the challenge of helping youth—and adults—replace interpersonal conflict with social harmony.

TIT FOR TAT

Humans are disposed to respond positively to those who treat them well, and negatively to those who show hostility. Some years ago, psychologists held a competition to create a computer program simulating human conflict. The winner was Canadian psychologist Anatol Rapaport (1960), who developed the "Tit for Tat" rule. The principle was very simple: *On the first encounter with another person, be cooperative. Then reciprocate the friendly or hostile reaction encountered.*

Humans are highly gregarious, curious, and sociable, and they seek opportunities for interaction. Tit for Tat offers a useful means of recruiting friends:

Tit: "Hi, you're new here, aren't you? My name is Joe." [Joe smiles.]

Tat: "Glad to meet you, Joe. They call me Stretch." [Stretch smiles.]

Tit: "We shoot hoops after school. Want to join us, Stretch?" [Joe smiles.]

Tat: "Awesome, Joe! I'll be there." [They exchange high fives.]

But a friendly nature could make an individual vulnerable if others have hostile intentions. Thus humans also have a self-protective option. At the first sign of danger or disrespect, we cease being friendly and display avoidant or threatening behavior:

Tit: "Hi! My name is Sue. Hope you like our school." [Sue smiles.]

Tat: "Don't count on it." [Newcomer scowls and looks away.]

Tit: "Well, I'm not wasting my time on you." [Sue walks off in a huff.]

Tat: "I can tell already that this school sucks." [Newcomer isolates.]

Tit for Tat worked well when humans lived among relatives in social harmony. It provided a better way for dealing with strangers than dueling with all aliens as enemies.

Because Tit for Tat operates across all cultures, it is probably embedded in the human genetic code. But people who cannot override genetic instructions are vulnerable (Csikszentmihalyi, 1990). In today's depersonalized, high-stress culture, humans live amidst strangers. The Tit for Tat rule is too limiting because tense encounters can easily escalate into violence. It is also morally suspect. Whereas the Golden Rule requires empathy, the Tit for Tat rule is a payback scheme.

Tit for Tat is also a profoundly inept strategy for the parenting, teaching, or treatment of challenging children. Winnicott (1965) observed that love and hate reactions are inevitable in work with children showing emotional problems. The challenge is to prevent a vicious cycle in which hate is answered with hate.

CONFLICT CYCLES

Nicholas Long developed the Conflict Cycle model for dealing with challenging behavior in schools, families, and treatment programs (Long & Morse, 1996). The Conflict Cycle describes how stress can escalate into crisis, drawing individuals into hostile confrontations. By understanding how the Tit for Tat process works, adults and youth are able to disengage from conflict cycles.

As shown in Figure 2.1 on page 28, a conflict cycle follows a four-station circular track: (1) A stressful event is perceived as a threat. This activates feelings and emotions. (2) Emotions prepare the person to take some action. For example, angry emotions cause a person to contemplate aggression. (3) The person engages in some coping behavior that may be either constructive or counterproductive. (4) Consequences of this

Figure 2.1
The Conflict Cycle

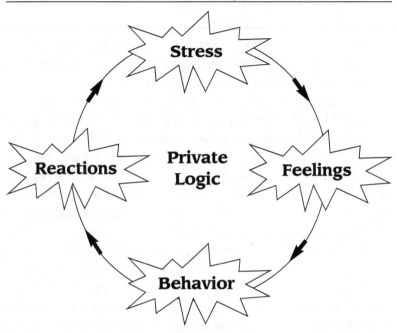

Stress is the perception of threat; it activates feelings, such as anger.

Feelings provide the motivation for behavior, such as aggression.

Behavior is a coping or defense strategy, such as verbal defiance.

Reactions include external consequences, inner feelings, and private logic.

Private logic is a person's unique pattern of perceiving and thinking.

© Circle of Courage

behavior include reactions from others as well as one's internal reactions. If these reactions de-escalate stress, the conflict cycle ends. But if the reactions heighten stress, one can expect another cycle around the track with increased intensity of emotions and behavior. The center of the conflict cycle is denoted *private logic,* the way a person perceives and thinks about his or her world.[1] At every stage, the person in conflict uses private logic to interpret and orchestrate responses.

People who encounter emotionally charged behavior pick up and recycle the same emotions in Tit for Tat fashion. Once ensnared in a conflict cycle, it is very difficult to extricate oneself. A feeling of "righteous rage" strongly motivates one to control or punish the adversary. Further, when youth show disruptive behavior, adults are in a double bind: To respond with coercion mirrors the youth's behavior, but backing away might reinforce the youth's coercive tactics (Reid, Patterson, & Snyder, 2002). There are better options than "fight or flight." The creative response to conflict is to show the youth better strategies for managing conflict.

Those who hope to teach others to manage conflict must first master these skills themselves. We sometimes demonstrate the Conflict Cycle to parents and professionals by showing clips from the movie *The Breakfast Club* (Hughes, 1985). In one scene, a trench coat–clad delinquent named Bender clashes with a macho principal, who is supervising several students in Saturday detention. The conflict cycle, as experienced by the principal, goes like this:

1. *Stress* came from the perceived threat: "This kid is defying my authority."

2. *Feelings* were triggered in the adult: "I am furious and won't take this crap!"

3. *Behavior* was the adult's macho threat display: "Don't mess with the bull!"

4. *Reaction* of the threatened youth included a volley of angry, defiant insults.

While other students watched in disbelief, the two combat-ants ratcheted up their emotional hostility. Each was enraged by the other, and neither would back down. In this lose-lose con-test, Bender was sentenced to many more weeks of Saturday detention, which the principal had to supervise. This comic por-trayal simulates real-world conflicts that are not at all funny.

Tit for Tat hostility is the prototype of a conflict cycle. A typ-ical conflict starts with a trivial disagreement and escalates into a series of provocations. Before one spike of anger dissi-pates, hostile barbs fuel an even higher surge of intense feel-ings. Unless someone disengages, this conflict can lead to emotional outbursts and violent actions (Zillman, 1993). A study of 100 violent incidents in New York City schools showed that most began as minor disagreements but escalated to dan-gerous levels when participants could not back away from conflict (Long, Fecser, & Brendtro, 1998).

Next, we track the conflict cycle across its four-station tra-jectory: (1) stress is triggered, (2) emotions are aroused, (3) behavior is goal directed, and (4) actions have consequences.

Stage 1: Stress Is Triggered

Stress is a state of heightened physical and psychological arousal. Stress results when a person perceives some situation as posing either a threat or a challenge (Lazarus & Folkman, 1984):

> *Threat is the perception of potential danger,* such as risk to safety, needs, goals, or self-worth. Threat triggers negative emotions, such as fear and anger.

> *Challenge is the perception of potential opportunity,* such as growth and mastery. Challenge triggers positive emotions, such as curiosity and excitement.

Threat and challenge are not opposites; many situations include both risk and opportunity. Further, what one individual sees as a threat, another may view as a challenge. Parachuting would cause extreme distress in most people, but a veteran skydiver experiences tremendous exhilaration. One person's crisis is another person's thrill.

The Conflict Cycle begins with some event that is perceived as a real or potential threat. Once the brain has made a threat appraisal, it triggers emotions that prep the person for "fight or flight" behavior.

There are many possible sources of stress (Long, Fecser, & Brendtro, 1998). *Developmental stress* arises from normal challenges of maturation. Even stable youth can be disrupted by the physical changes of adolescence and conflicts surrounding independence and intimacy. *Environmental stress* involves challenging physical and social situations. Some children live in poverty, lack food and clothing, are sleep deprived, and experience health problems. *Psychological stress* results from frustrations at meeting basic psychological needs. Children experience loss, rejection, failure, helplessness, and hopelessness. Intrusive behavior management can also cause severe stress.

Stress is a factor underlying most emotional and behavioral disorders (Bradley, 2000). Diverse therapies all seek to reduce distress and strengthen coping strategies. Likewise, many medications are effective across disorders in reducing emotional agitation and distress. Therapy may redesign the connections of the brain, particularly the areas that control fear and aggression.

Children labeled "emotionally disturbed" do not cope with stress in adaptive ways (Murphy, 1961). Treatment interventions for these children seek to keep stress at manageable levels. In contrast, "shock treatment" environments such as boot camps seek to impose overwhelming stress to make subjects pliable to obedience training. A precursor to effective intervention is to manage stress so that calm and reason can prevail. When stress is at the level of "just manageable difficulty," children are challenged toward mastery (Hobbs, 1994).

Whenever life's difficulties pose a threat, the resulting stress unleashes powerful emotions. Psychiatrist M. Scott Peck (1978) begins his book *The Road Less Traveled* with the profound understatement "Life is difficult." Some teens wear more colorful slogans emblazoned on T-shirts proclaiming, "S—t Happens."

Stage 2: Emotions Are Aroused

Stress activates emotions that in turn drive behavior. We use the term *feelings* to describe the subjective experience of emotions. The word *emotion* shares the same root as the word *motivation*. Emotions trigger a range of internal changes that motivate specific patterns of coping behavior (Nathanson, 1992). Thus anger primes the body for an immediate, short-term burst of energy. The brain also keys an angry person to remain in a stressed state for hours after the end of the conflict. One isolated episode can carry over to later, unrelated situations (Zillman, 1993).

Emotions register on our faces, giving others some idea of how we are feeling so they know how to act toward us. Charles Darwin (1872/1988) discovered that humans have inborn capacities to express and interpret emotions; facial expressions signal the same emotions across different cultures. He noted that emotions reveal our intentions more accurately than words, which can be falsified.

Emotional intelligence is the ability to monitor the feelings of oneself and others and to use this information for successful social behavior (Salovey, Hsee, & Mayer, 1993). The pinnacle of emotional intelligence is empathy, the ability to tune in to the emotions of another. By age five, most children can interpret emotions accurately. Once they recognize that others can read their emotions, children develop skills of deception, masking feelings with disguised facial expressions. This is not necessarily dishonesty; it is sometimes a good idea to act nice even though you are mad, and to hold back tears even though you are hurt.

Hundreds of terms in everyday language describe the subtleties of emotion. Researchers focus on fewer than 10 emotional patterns thought to have unique pathways in the brain. Commonly studied negative emotions include fear, anger, anxiety, sadness, shame, and disgust. These unpleasant emotional states motivate avoidance or attack behavior.

Many negative emotions have counterparts in positive emotions (Plutchik, 1980). These include affection, joy, and pride. Some researchers add sympathy and gratitude to the list of uniquely human emotions (Pinker, 1997). Aristotle identified similar "human affections," and his list also included courage and charity (Alexander & Selesnick, 1966). Positive emotions generally motivate prosocial approach behavior, including helpfulness and generosity (Isen, 2000).

The most pervasive positive emotion is one that most do not even think of as an emotion: *curiosity* or *interest.* The desire to explore and learn is foremost in the mind of an alert, healthy, unthreatened person (Izard & Ackerman, 2000). People wrapped up in concentration and creativity are in a state called "flow" (Csikszentmihalyi, 1996). Problem solving is intrinsically rewarding and motivates learning (Dewey, 1913). Sir Isaac Newton described the curiosity emotion: "I seem to have been only a boy playing on the seashore, and diverting myself in now and then finding a smoother pebble or a prettier shell than ordinary, whilst the great ocean of truth lay all undiscovered before me" (Van Doren, 1991, p. 209).

Stage 3: Behavior Is Goal Directed

All behavior functions to create some change in the person or environment. For simplicity, we will use the term *goal* to suggest that—at some level—all behavior has purpose. For nearly a century, psychologists have distinguished two types of learning: *operant conditioning* (a dog jumping through a hoop to get a biscuit) and *classical conditioning* (Pavlov's dog reflexively salivating at the sound of a bell). Operant conditioning occurs in the higher problem-solving brain, whereas classical conditioning involves the emotional brain. But brain research has shown that the two types of learning are interconnected and influence goal-directed behavior (Gallagher, 2000).

Positive and negative emotions both are powerful motivators for human behavior. At infancy, humans react instinctually as emotions drive behavior. As the rational brain becomes a bigger player, children employ language and coping behaviors to solve problems and manage emotions (Epstein & Meier, 1989). Maturity brings a sophisticated range of coping strategies (Hauser & Bowlds, 1990).

Human brains are designed for problem solving. When we are not facing problems, we invent them, working on puzzles, hobbies, and games or solving conflicts vicariously through novels or movies. In 1926, Russian psychologist Bluma Zeigarnik made an important discovery that has become known as the *Zeigarnik effect*. The brain cannot let go of unsolved problems and is highly motivated to determine possible solutions. If we cannot immediately resolve a problem, we may put it aside for a while, but even then the brain keeps scanning for solutions. We dream about unresolved conflicts and sometimes wake up with the solution. After Einstein determined that classic theories of physics were mistaken, he was in a state of stress for the next seven years, trying to solve the puzzle of the universe (Fromm, 1998).

Problem solving is the constructive means of coping with stress, whereas problem behavior represents a breakdown in this process (Dewey, 1933; Torrance, 1965). Children choose coping responses that they believe to have the best chances of success. Strategies that worked in the past are likely to be repeated. Behaviors that have been repeated many times become automatic, and people do not have to preplan their responses. Old habits can persist even though they no longer serve a purpose.[2] For example, a child under stress may regress to tattling and clinging behavior that once brought adult attention, even though this infantile behavior now produces only peer ridicule.

An example of coping behavior is seen in children's attempts to deal with the threat of abandonment. The fear of rejection and loss of love leads to a series of problem-solving strategies. A typical sequence is protest, despair, and detachment (Lazarus & Folkman, 1984). Initially, children try to get the attention of adults by expressing affection or crying. If this fails, they may convert their frustration to rage or retreat into despair. Some completely detach from adults and avoid future relationships altogether.

Behavioral goals are closely related to a person's needs, emotions, motives, and values. In a broad sense, goals either *seek* or *avoid* something. Humans engage in purposeful behavior to survive, maintain emotional balance, and optimize growth. These goal categories are summarized as follows.[3]

Survival Goals

Seek safety, sustenance, health, and propagation.

Avoid danger, deprivation, illness, and extinction.

Emotional Goals

Seek enjoyment, interest, excitement, and tranquility.

Avoid distress, boredom, irritation, and overarousal.

Growth Goals

Seek belonging, mastery, independence, and generosity.

Avoid alienation, failure, powerlessness, and purpose-lessness.

Problems result from pursuing the wrong goals or using the wrong strategies to reach legitimate goals. Lois Murphy (1961) of the Menninger Foundation identified various strategies children use to cope with stress. Constructive coping includes prioritizing, creatively problem solving, persisting, and if a situation cannot be changed, learning to adapt and "put up with it." Those unable to cope constructively employ defensive "fight or flight" behavior.

Children whose basic needs are frustrated experience extreme stress; unable to cope effectively, they are overwhelmed by crisis. Psychiatrist Bruce Perry has studied victims of extreme trauma, such as children from the Waco cult of David Koresh. Perry found that brain maturation can be slowed by early trauma. Such children use more primitive styles of problem solving—often employing aggression as a coping tool (Perry & Pollard, 1997).

The same coping behavior can be motivated by different emotions and goals. Thus there are various kinds of "fight" behavior, including reactive and proactive aggression (Zillman, 1993). In *reactive aggression*, anger is the core emotion. A person feels violated and responds by attacking someone believed to be at blame. Because these actions often occur in the heat of hostile interactions, the solution is to de-escalate the anger, such as by conflict resolution. In contrast, *proactive aggression* is driven not by anger but by a lack of the positive emotions of caring and empathy. Thus a bully is not upset but enjoys seeing a victim dominated and terrorized. Peers reinforce such "recreational bullying," giving the bully a sense of power. Regardless of the cause of aggression, adults need to intervene, but the type of intervention may depend on the goal of the behavior.

Self-injury is another behavior with diverse causes. Polly Nichols (2000) notes that self-mutilation has become more common among girls. Many hurt themselves without awareness of pain; endorphins are released, resulting in an emotional high that blocks out intolerable stress. Other acts of mutilation stem from faulty private logic, reflected in beliefs such as "My body is disgusting" or "I deserve punishment." Some self-mutilate to gain attention from others, but this behavior should not be dismissed as simple "manipulation." A particularly troubling motive for mutilation among girls is to belong to a particular group who cut or burn themselves. Without identification of the reason behind such behavior, the means of effective management can be elusive.

Stage 4: Actions Have Consequences

All behavior has consequences. These include natural consequences, reactions from others, and internal reactions in thoughts or feelings. In general, behavior managers seek to strengthen or reduce behavior by administering positive or unpleasant consequences. Manipulating rewards and punishments works with many youngsters, particularly younger children and those who seek adult social reinforcement. But imposing consequences can backfire with youth who resent adult influence. In such cases, attempts to reward or punish behavior can lead to avoidance or "counter-control."

A basic principle of psychology is that behavior functions to achieve certain effects or consequences. This principle is not as simple as it sounds:

• Consequences can be immediate or long term.

- The same consequence can have different effects on different children.
- Many behaviors produce mixed negative and positive consequences.
- Adult consequences may compete with the reinforcement power of peers.
- Consequences resulting from private logic or feelings are hard to detect.
- Youth are not always aware of why they persist in certain behavior.

All behavior is purposeful, even if it seems senseless to others. Sometimes the goal of the behavior is apparent from observation, such as when a bully shakes down weaker peers to get their money. At other times the function of the behavior is unclear. If we don't understand the goal or purpose of a youth's behavior, we may employ interventions that only make matters worse.

Some youth persist in patterns of self-defeating behavior. Neither punishment nor natural consequences are effective in changing their behavior. But behavior is purposeful, so if there is no external payoff, then to understand the behavior, we need to know what is going on in the young person's mind.

THE AGITATED MIND

B. F. Skinner (1953) proposed that scientific psychology could deal only with observable behavior. The brain was viewed as a "black box," and to be concerned with the "inner life" was speculative and unscientific. But psychologists have long been interested in the broader triad of behavior, thinking, and feeling. Advances in brain research and cognitive psychology are yielding important new facts about how thoughts and feelings affect observable behavior. Surface behavior represents only part of the picture. As our colleague Mark Freado says, we must look beyond the outside kid and discover the inside kid. In this section, we review recent research that sheds light on the agitated inner mind of a child in conflict.

The Amygdala: The Brain's Danger Detector

To understand how our emotions work, it is necessary to understand a brain structure called the amygdala. This is because the amygdala (the name literally means almond) is involved in the ways that our likes and dislikes are formed, how our emotions affect our actions and our memories, and how we interact socially with others.

—John P. Aggleton (2000, preface)

The amygdala (pronounced uh-MIG-duh-luh) is the brain's danger detector.[4] This structure, shaped like a pair of almonds, is located in the emotional brain, inward from the temples. The amygdala's job is to constantly scan all senses for any emotionally charged data.[5] This alert sentry is on the lookout for anything "important, interesting, attractive, fearful, distressing, irritating" (Kusché & Greenberg, in press, p. 5). The amygdala is a central screening system that connects to autonomic, hormonal, motor, and higher brain functions. Within a few milliseconds of perceiving a stimulus, the amygdala makes a tentative decision about whether approach or avoidance is the best plan. Even before the higher brain knows what is happening, the amygdala can activate defenses.

The amygdala is the linchpin of the emotional brain.[6] The brain has three parts with different tasks: (1) The *brain stem* handles basic survival functions in all animals and is also known as the reptilian brain. (2) In mammals, the *limbic brain* is wrapped in a ring around the brain stem. This is the brain's emotional command center, triggering feelings and storing emotional memories. (3) In humans, the *prefrontal brain,* or neocortex, is highly developed to handle complex thought and problem solving. The adult human brain is 90 percent prefrontal brain and 10 percent limbic brain. This ratio is reversed in rabbits.

Besides detecting danger, the amygdala keeps a permanent archive of important, highly arousing life events. When we experience powerful positive or negative emotions, the amygdala temporarily stores these memories and then projects them to other areas of the brain for long-term storage. Memories formed in a single emotionally charged event can last a lifetime in what is termed "permastore." In this permastore, the amygdala keeps a permanent reference of memories about events that brought extremes of emotion, such as fear or joy. This is why learning tied to positive emotions is more enduring. But vivid, terrifying events are also seared into our brain circuitry and cannot be forgotten.

Stress triggers a surge of brain chemicals that store emotional memories. These are stored in verbal and nonverbal formats in different areas of the brain (LeDoux, 1996). The amygdala imprints emotional memories. Though conditioned fears may not be conscious, they can be disabling. Other areas of the brain keep detailed records of emotional events that can be recalled and verbalized. Thus a child may vividly recall specific details of abuse.[7] Not all emotional memories can be recalled. When distress is too extreme or prolonged, the brain can create other chemicals that block memories.

In general, once emotional memories are stored in the emotional brain, this information is retained unless reprogrammed by the verbal brain. This is one of the purposes of talk therapy. The higher human brain is also involved in positive emotional learning, which includes curiosity, concentration, insight, self-concept, empathy, and altruism. Emotional distress can interfere with this emotional learning. Because the rational brain manages emotions, brain dysfunction can dramatically impair social behavior.

The amygdala specializes in reading emotional cues from the human face, and a person whose amygdala has been removed cannot interpret emotions such as fear, anger, or disgust. The human face is endowed with dozens of muscles whose only purpose is to signal an emotional state (Nathanson, 1992). The sight of fear, anger, or distress displayed on the face of another person can trigger intense emotional responses.

The eyes send potent emotional messages monitored by the amygdala. Being able to detect when the eyes of others are trained on us provides important survival information. Hostile, piercing eyes communicate an invasive display of threat. When experiencing the emotion of shame, we sense that the eyes of others are turned on us with disapproval, and we want to hide our face to avert their glance. Children with autism and those who have been conditioned to fear adults often find eye contact threatening and respond with gaze aversion and withdrawal behavior. Aggressive youth are often hypervigilant in their search for cues of hostility, and even casual eye contact can be misconstrued as a threat. On the other hand, we communicate positive emotions with warm facial expressions and friendly eye contact. With those we trust and like, eye contact invites social bonding. Among the most intimate emotional exchanges is interocular contact, when two people look deep into each other's eyes.

The amygdala is involved in a full range of emotional and behavioral disorders. Fear, anxiety, aggression, mood, attention, and addiction are all influenced by the amygdala. In PTSD, emotionally charged memories are imprinted in the brain, and subsequent stressful stimuli can trigger overwhelming feelings of fear like those associated with the initial trauma (Pynoos, Steinberg, & Wraith, 1995). The amygdala becomes so excitable that even low levels of stimulation cause "kindling," in which the amygdala unleashes a torrent of brain activity not unlike a seizure. In addiction, mere exposure to stimuli associated with prior drug use can trigger powerful cravings resulting in relapse.

Children's brains have an operating amygdala at birth, so emotionally charged memories can predate language. Years later, emotional memories outside of conscious awareness still can trigger strong emotions (Goleman, 1995). The brain's ability to manage emotions develops slowly during childhood. With inner speech, children gain significant control over their emotional responses. However, the emotional brain continues to exert powerful influence, recruiting reason in the service of their feelings (Izard & Ackerman, 2000). There is no such thing as a purely "rational" response; the brain always operates with both a stream of thought and a stream of feeling. Emotions of fear and aggression can distort thinking and produce conflict in relationships.

Angry Private Logic

In the classic book *Children Who Hate,* Fritz Redl and David Wineman (1951) document the distorted private logic of youngsters in conflict. Basing their findings on thousands of hours of direct observation, they describe in rich detail the thinking errors of youth with emotional and behavioral problems. Subsequent research has shown that these children view their world as unfriendly and dangerous, and they may react to the slightest provocation with hostility (Dodge, 1993).

Certain youths are more easily provoked to anger than others. Children with attention deficit/hyperactivity disorder (ADHD) are easily excitable. Delinquents may be daring and risk taking and put fewer restraints on aggression. Alcohol and other drugs can cripple brain functions so that reasoning cannot regulate emotional agitation. Intoxicated people are less restrained by anticipation of consequences, and their aggression can reach dangerous levels, such as in continuing to fight a victim who is not fighting back.

Behavior that seems senseless to the outside observer often makes perfect sense in the private logic of the youth. One girl told us she baits authority figures so they will get upset because "I want them to be as miserable as I am." Another youth defied his principal because he felt he was being treated unfairly. A seven-year-old boy brought a gun to school because his mother was in prison, and he thought he would be sent there with her. Another child gets so emotionally wound up that temper tantrums operate to release tension, even if this behavior leads to punishment. A youth in a residential setting acted up when release was imminent so he would not have to return to an abusive home. There is such a rich variety of private logic that the best way to understand behavior is to know what a youth is thinking.

Cognitive psychologist John Gibbs and colleagues have identified four major patterns of thinking errors of youth in conflict (Gibbs, Potter, & Goldstein, 1995). They avoid describing these patterns as "pathological thinking" or "criminal thinking" because all humans are susceptible to these four distortions in thinking:

Self-centered thinking is shown by persons so wrapped up in their own needs and emotions that they are unresponsive to the needs or feelings of others: "When I get mad, somebody is going to get hurt."

Blaming is attacking others for their faults. It is common among youth who lack empathy for others and shift responsibility for their own problems onto others: "He deserves to be beaten up; nobody can stand him."

Assuming the worst is a tendency toward a negative bias, such as believing that others are hostile: "You cannot trust anybody because they will just stab you in the back."

Minimizing and mislabeling are rationalizations that play down one's own problem behavior and even justify it: "School's boring, so we decided to have fun and raise a little hell."

Gibbs (1994) describes egotism as the primary thinking error and empathy as the ultimate measure of moral maturity. The lack of close experience with empathic adults blocks the development of empathy, particularly in boys without a caring father figure (Cohn, 1996).

Bullying and exploitation of others is seen as an "empathy deficit." Youth need corrective experiences to stimulate empathy and helping behavior (Olweus, 1996). Punishment only reinforces their bias that the world is hostile and respect must be gained by threat and coercion (Beck, 1999). Some youths describe their antisocial acts in a nonchalant or braggadocio fashion and show little remorse for their actions. This does not establish them as psychopaths without human concern. Such tough talk may be an attempt to keep from feeling guilty. Distorted private logic enables youths to trick themselves. They minimize problems, blame others, and paint victims in dehumanizing terms. This thinking pattern masks the painful awareness that they have seriously hurt a fellow human (Gibbs, Potter, Goldstein, & Brendtro, 1996, 1998).

Thinking patterns can be difficult to change because life experience weaves an interlocking web of beliefs and behavior. Carol Gilligan and colleagues describe the outspoken, confrontational manner of "loud black girls." Anita's voice conveys a private logic of defiance designed to cope with a hostile world:

> We don't take no kind of b.s. from nobody. That's how we
> are . . . we don't care who you are, black girls don't take
> no kind of trash from nobody . . . a lot of my girlfriends
> that are white, they take a lot of trash from a lot of people,
> and I sit there like, hmm, what's your problem? Why are
> you taking that? . . . we're very blunt . . . we don't bite our
> tongues for anybody, you know. (Taylor, Gilligan, &
> Sullivan, 1996, p. 72)

Such thinking projects a defensive strength and perhaps protects against abuse. It can also be self-defeating if it evokes hostile reactions from peers and authority. Still, this style of thinking and behavior has produced some payoffs. Criticism and punishment seldom cause defiant youth to change their biased worldview, but only confirm and strengthen it.

When a youth's behavior is driven by angry private logic, arbitrary consequences are often counterproductive. Unless entrenched thinking can be understood and altered, children may continue self-defeating behavior, whatever the cost. A punished child may keep fighting adults with the irrational belief "They think they can mess with me. I will show them." Some kids would spit all the way to the electric chair just to spite those in authority.

Children need help putting aside immature and self-serving logic. This requires adults who recognize the needs of the youth, even in the face of disturbed and disruptive behavior. Unfortunately, as the Tit for Tat principle suggests, adults often respond to troubling behavior with threat. This threat triggers their thinking errors, emotional reactions, and rash disciplinary interventions.

"ARE YOU GOING TO MAKE ME?"
Theo's Threat

Theo is a middle school youth from a biracial background.[8] Since kindergarten, he has attended all-white schools. He still vividly recalls the first day he eagerly started school, only to be called "the N word" by peers. Although he wants friends, Theo has developed a belligerent response to being bullied. He will not back down from conflict, even if confronted by bigger peers.

We first met Theo when he and a group of older peers were charged with breaking into the home of an elderly man to rob him. Theo was not directly involved but waited in the car. When he discovered the man had been beaten, he was very upset, but he initially did not tell on the other boys because they were the only friends he had.

In preparing a Developmental Audit (see Chapter 8) for the juvenile court, we reviewed his school records. In spite of conflict with peers, Theo got along reasonably well with many of his teachers in the elementary grades. In middle school, ongoing conflict with peers led to his being labeled by teachers as a troublemaker. We located the following behavior incident report completed by a fifth-grade social studies teacher (Van Bockern, 2000). Here is his account of the incident.

I confronted Theo and asked him why he wasn't participating in his group and why he wasn't doing the assigned activity. He responded that his group didn't want him to. I said that wasn't true and it didn't matter if they did or not; he should participate.

Later, Theo stood up and confronted another student by saying, "Are you going to make me?" I stepped in and said, "Yes, I am going to make you sit down." I told him that he wasn't going to start anything in my class. He said he'd do anything he pleased; he didn't need us or this class. Theo got angrier and angrier while I tried to get him to sit down.

Theo then erupted and told me, "F— you!" I then grabbed him to sit him down. He in turn pushed me and put his fists up and wanted to fight. He said, "No one f—-in' touches me," and started calling me out to fight. He said he would kick my ass and wanted to go. I told him to get into my office. He kept refusing and swearing at me and asking me to fight.

Beginning to get very upset, I grabbed for him to push him into my office. He again pushed me away and said not to touch him and continued to try to get me to fight. He slowly made his way into my office, where I told him to sit down. Theo continued to yell and swear at me and kept trying to get me to fight. At this time, he said he was going to get a gun and shoot me! He promised that he would get me somehow, some way.

———

This incident is a classic example of what Nicholas Long calls "the Double Struggle" (Long, Wood, & Fecser, 2001). The teacher struggled both to control an angry student and to control his own emotions. He failed on both counts. In recent surveys of teachers, over 90 percent report that they do not feel competent to handle crisis situations. This is not surprising because this topic rarely has been given serious attention in teacher education programs. The untrained adult reacts to crisis as a threat, and this triggers a conflict cycle. As pioneering school psychologist John Morgan (1936) noted, a high degree of emotional tension in an adult is a good index of relative incompetence to deal with the situation at hand.

NOTES

[1] Alfred Adler first used the term *private logic* to describe the unique way each child completes this series: "I am____; others are____; the world is____; therefore____." This self-talk is based on an elaborate system of beliefs and is thought to be a kind of here-and-now private dialogue—in effect, inner speech (Vygotsky, 1962). With some differences in emphasis, private logic has been described with terms such as *self-talk, scripts, schemas, mental maps, internal models,* and *the whispering self.*

[2] Gordon Allport (1937) called such behaviors "functionally autonomous." B. F. Skinner (1953) noted that responses that were accidentally reinforced can continue as "superstitious behavior."

[3] Adapted from the taxonomy of the interpersonal goals developed by Ford and Nichols (Goldstein & Martens, 2000).

[4] This discussion draws from LeDoux (1996), Aggleton (2000), and Kusché and Greenberg (in press).

[5] Although most research on the amygdala has dealt with its role in the emotion of fear, the amygdala is thought to be involved in approach behavior as well, including sexuality, hunger, and addiction. Because of our focus on conflict, this discussion emphasizes the amygdala's role in the detection of danger or threat.

[6] The emotional brain, or limbic system, also includes the *thalamus,* which is a relay station for outside stimulation; the *hypothalamus,* which is a relay station for internal bodily sensation; and the *hippocampus,* which stores the details of emotionally charged memories that can be retrieved by language.

[7] This detailed memory is stored in the hippocampus as well as in areas of the higher brain (LeDoux, 1996).

[8] This assessment was prepared under the direction of Steve Van Bockern of Reclaiming Youth International. The name and identifying information are altered, but the teacher's report is reproduced as it was written.

CHAPTER THREE

Pathways to Problems

Terrible tragedies are inflicted on many children during the early developmental years which plant time bombs that go off later in life.

—J. F. Masterson (1981, p. 187)

This chapter identifies various patterns of discordant relationships that can launch a child on a trajectory of self-defeating behavior. Psychiatrist Gerald Edelstien (1990) notes that most explanations for childhood emotional and behavioral problems are *trauma* theories, whether or not the word *trauma* is used. Basically, something went wrong in the developmental process, and it had a damaging effect on emotional and behavioral adjustment. He defines trauma as some stressful experience that produces very painful feelings, causing the individual to adopt defensive or coping behaviors to protect against a reoccurrence.

Trauma can lead to virtually any externalizing or internalizing disorder. The most direct diagnosis is PTSD. This pattern of symptoms includes hypervigilance, blunted emotions, and the tendency to relive past traumas in memory or action. One young person described this experience as follows: "I get overwhelmed and confused. I don't know if I should run or fight or even who the enemy might be." The behavior of many youth who have been traumatized is given other labels, such as conduct disorder, oppositional defiant disorder, attachment disorder, depression, or delinquency. These describe patterns of behavior but do not reveal much about the underlying problems of children in conflict.

By adolescence, they are living in a constant state of frightened preparedness for yet another round with pain or terror. What we see then is the reckless, hostile, "acting-out behaviors." . . . Frequently, an implicit consensus evolves among mental health professionals, school personnel, juvenile justice staff, and parents that these kids are beyond help. At 12 or 14 or 16 years of age, we have given up on them. In response, they give up on us and on themselves. (Echo Bridge Productions, 1996, p. 3)

Humans are highly resilient, and many traumatic events can be outgrown or overcome. After World War II, psychologists worked with millions of children who had witnessed severe trauma and loss. Treatment did not usually involve causing the child to relive painful memories. Instead, the goal was to help the child feel safe and learn to live in peace and harmony (Diel, 1987). Therapy also may heal trauma by altering brain structures as emotionally charged memories are edited and revised, lessening the person's sense of danger or insecurity (Ross, 2000; Eisenberg, 2001).

In the following discussion, we consider three broad types of damaging experience. These include trauma resulting from misattunement in behavior management, childhood maltreatment, and destructive treatment interventions.

MISATTUNEMENT

The lifetime emotional costs of lack of attunement in childhood can be great.

—Daniel Goleman (1995, p. 102)

A youth says, "I could tell from the vibes that I could trust her." This is *attunement,* individuals operating in harmony with the emotional rhythm of one another. A youth who says, "I just couldn't connect with that person," is describing *misattunement.* This discord can arise even in infancy if a parent is not responsive to the child's feelings. Misattunement is highly stressful and creates conflictual relationships.

Attunement requires the emotional capacity of empathy. The brain's amygdala tracks subtle cues in order to recognize and adapt to another person's feelings. As with all capacities, people are not equally adept at empathy. And when we are emotionally agitated—as in the heat of anger—none of us is likely to show much empathy (Goleman, 1995).

Most behavioral problems are not the result of abuse from adults. Rather, there is misattunement between the needs of the child and the behavior management style of the adult. This includes problems of temperament as well as the use of intrusive discipline methods.

Difficult Temperament

Even the most concerned and responsible parent can be challenged by a child with a "difficult" temperament. Ken and Andrea McCluskey, both educators, describe their frustrations in dealing with a high-octane child, Amber:

> From the beginning, Amber got into all sorts of trouble. It was necessary to supervise her virtually every second. For example, it was impossible to turn one's back while bathing Amber. If left to her own devices for even a moment, she would be climbing on the sink, leaping to the curtain rod, and attempting to hang upside-down by her knees. The possibilities for disaster were legion. In games like hide-and-seek, for example, Amber would do ill-judged things such as conceal herself in the oven. If we had ever relaxed our vigilance (by pre-heating without looking), we might well have ended up with cooked Amber. Once Amber hit the public school system, all hell broke loose—it was Hiroshima revisited. After her first few days in kindergarten, we were told that Amber was not ready for school. The teacher asked, in wild panic, "Don't you think you should keep her home?" That's a fine start, having a daughter who is virtually expelled from kindergarten. When we resisted this notion, a social worker was sent out to discover what form of abuse we were inflicting on this poor child (not realizing it was quite the opposite). In probing for information, the social worker asked, "Do you love her?" Mom's response, "Of course I love her. Look at her. Would I have kept her if I didn't?" (McCluskey & McCluskey, 2001, pp. 34–36)

Drawing from a vast lottery of possible human traits, children display markedly different temperaments. Temperament refers to stable patterns of personality and behavior, usually visible from early childhood. According to the "goodness of fit" model of Thomas and Chess (1977), discord arises when the characteristics of the child are not in sync with demands of the environment. Some children are temperamentally active. If they are raised in households and classrooms where noise and activity are welcome, no maladaptive behavior results. But if they are reared in an environment where quiet, polite behavior is valued, discord results.

There are two possible solutions to a mismatch of temperament. One is to try to change the child, typically by using medication or behavioral modification. The other is to match child and environment—for example, by placement with a teacher whose temperament can accommodate the child (Lewis, 2000). Although psychoactive medications may limit the symptoms, the more basic solution is to improve the goodness of fit between child and environment (Chess & Thomas, 1986).

Differences in temperament have some biological basis but are also shaped by learning. Those most commonly researched include tendencies toward *extraversion, anxiety, aggression,* and *affiliation* (Derryberry & Rothbart, 1997). British researcher Eysenck (1970) has extensively studied extraversion, which is a combination of sociability, spontaneity, and adventurousness. He has also researched anxious and inhibited behavior, which he calls neuroticism. At first glance, extraversion seems to be a strength and neuroticism a weakness. But a youth high on extraversion and low on anxiety has few internal restraints on behavior. Such children may become aggressive, impulsive, and risk seeking (Eysenck, 1997). In contrast, children with anxious temperaments may actually adapt better because they are able to inhibit impulsive behavior.

ADHD, the most common "behavior disorder," may well be a variation in temperament, one end of a continuum of normal behavior (Levy, Hay, McStephen, Wood, & Waldman, 1997). These children show some combination of distractibility, hyperactivity, and impulsivity. Who is labeled ADHD depends on where one draws the line between "normal" and "disordered." Thus estimates of the incidence of ADHD range from 4 percent to over 20 percent (Anastopoulos & Shaffer, 2001; Nolan, Gadow, & Sprafkin, 2001). But if one in five boys shows ADHD traits, this may indicate rambunctiousness rather than pathology. Typical behavior for many boys includes curiosity, contrariness, and difficulty staying on task. This is exactly how many creative people act when forced to perform boring, repetitive tasks (Kipnis, 1999).

The ADHD label scoops up a diverse group of youngsters, but the precise cause of this behavior is usually unclear. Anxiety, trauma, and sexual abuse can produce attention problems and alter brain functioning. So can brain injury, but most children with ADHD show no obvious neurological dysfunction, though they may benefit from medication that helps them focus (Pliszka, Carlson, & Swanson, 1999; Forness, Kavale, & Crenshaw, 1999). Like many other temperament variations, ADHD runs in families (Anastopoulos & Shaffer, 2001). This does not mean that parents passed along bad genes. Sociobiologists remind us that a diverse genetic pool is needed for survival of a species. In hunter-gatherer cultures, kids with behaviors we call ADHD probably would have made the best scouts and hunters. Today's sedentary school requirements turn this talent into trouble.

Youthful behaviors that irritate many adults reflect generational differences in temperament. Kids are noisy and rowdy and explore the outer limits of propriety. If a group of adults acted this uninhibited, we would presume they were drunk. Brain research shows that youthful impulsivity is related to immature brain development. Before 17 to 19 years of age, many youths cannot fully use the executive functions of the brain to manage emotions (Murray, 1998).

Youthful exuberance can easily be confused with psychopathology. Before Fritz Redl opened a program for aggressive children at the National Institute of Mental Health, he prepared his staff by bringing a Boy Scout troop to live in the facility on a weekend "camp-in." As the scouts bounced off the walls and sprayed water around the washrooms, staff got a "baseline" of normal problems that occur when high-energy youth encounter the lures of a psychiatric ward. A century ago, Jane Addams worked with youth from the streets of Chicago. She described their tendency to become emotionally aroused and plunge into reckless behavior. Her diagnosis for this disorder was "the spirit of adventure."

Intrusive Discipline

What do children need from adults? To sum up decades of study in two words, the answer is love and limits. The first involves affection, acceptance, and kindness—there is no debate here. Limits are more complicated. A lack of boundaries and adult guidance is tantamount to neglect. But both authoritarian and overprotective child rearing interfere with emotional growth.

Recent youth development research makes a sharp distinction between *behavioral* control and *psychological* control (Barber & Harmon, 2002):

Behavioral control involves monitoring a child to teach responsibility. Without guidance and supervision, children are exposed to a host of developmental dangers. The adult respects a child's emotional needs and adjusts supervision as the youngster gains self-control.

Psychological control involves manipulating the child's feelings, relationships, and self-expression. Psychological control is coercive, hostile, invalidating, possessive, and sometimes overprotecting. The adult does not respect the young person's need to develop identity and autonomy.

Behavioral control is a developmental *asset,* whereas psychological control is a developmental *liability.* Psychological control is called *intrusive* because it stifles self-development (Bradley, 2000). These are common techniques of intrusive discipline that employ psychological control:

Withdrawal of love makes the adult's affection or attention dependent on a child's behaving or being as the caregiver wishes.

Instilling shame whips around the emotions and self-worth of the child (Nelson & Quick, 2002).

Stirring up anxiety or fear keeps the youngster off guard and uncertain about the adult's intentions.

Forbidding expression of disagreement deprives the child of a sense of autonomy.

Isolating the child from outside influence or relationships is saying, in effect, "I own you."

Overprotecting and infantilizing blocks the development of responsible independence.

Intrusive discipline by adults models the use of "relational aggression" as a way of handling conflict (Nelson & Quick, 2002). Youth treated in this manner often use similar methods in dealing with siblings or peers. Girls can become proficient at manipulative retaliation, using rumor and social exclusion and sabotaging friendships. Boys often use verbal put-downs in psychological warfare against those they bully. Ridicule can be even more damaging than physical assault because insults are frontal attacks on self-worth.

Whether intrusive controls are wielded by parent, teacher, sibling, peer, or institution, the findings appear to be consistent: Psychological control interferes with the development of autonomy (Barber, Bean, & Erickson, 2002). This is seen in the lack of self-reliance, self-expression, decision making, achievement, and self-worth. Youth who do not learn to control themselves show a full range of problems from self-destructive behavior to aggression.

MALTREATMENT

In a typical year, about three million children in the United States are reported to child protective services as alleged victims of maltreatment. Maltreatment increases the risk of problems in adolescence, including school problems, emotional and mental health disorders, substance abuse, and delinquency (Kelley, Thornberry, & Smith, 1997). It is no coincidence that three million children yearly also come in contact with the juvenile justice system. Often these statistics track children at different stages of development. Once an abused youth becomes a juvenile offender, concern about public safety leads to punitive responses, which place the youth at risk of further victimization (Kelley, Thornberry, & Smith, 1997).

Categories of Cruelty

The term *child maltreatment* encompasses a broad spectrum of destructive child-rearing environments. In general, maltreatment includes physical, sexual, and psychological abuse and neglect. Much maltreatment never comes to the attention of authorities, but according to one source, maltreatment affects 14 percent of a typical population of children prior to age 12 (Kelley, Thornberry, & Smith, 1997). Maltreatment is correlated with a host of problems, including delinquency, teen pregnancy, drug use, difficulties in school, and psychiatric disorders. However, long-term developmental damage is not inevitable if protective factors are in place to buffer the child and boost resiliency.

The most difficult form of maltreatment to document is psychological abuse. Garbarino and Eckenrode (1997) identify these patterns that can be found in families, schools, and residential settings:

Spurning: demeaning, rejecting, and showing hostility

Terrorizing: making direct threats and placing a child in danger

Isolating: restricting social contact or placing a child in seclusion

Corrupting: ignoring or encouraging self-harm or deviant acts

Denying emotional needs: failing to give respect and affection

Withholding treatment: ignoring mental health and educational needs

There has been an explosion of research on the damaging effects of maltreatment.[1] Physical and sexual abuse can create chemical differences in the human brain. Maltreated children live in a chronic state of tension. In stressful situations, they show a wariness or hypervigilance not found in normal children. Maltreated children are less able to manage hostility. It might seem that physically abused children would become "used to" aggression and desensitized to it. In fact, the opposite is true. They become much more emotionally aroused and angered when they encounter aggression (Cicchetti & Lynch, 1995).

Children who show delinquent behavior before adolescence are usually victims of maltreatment. The Child Welfare League of America studied children known to child protection agencies in Sacramento. The arrest rate among children referred to child welfare agencies was 67 times higher than the arrest rate among children not known to the child welfare system. Of course, most maltreated children do not become delinquents (Petit & Brooks, 1998).

Being reared in alcohol-abusing families makes children 5 times more likely to be physically neglected and 10 times more likely to be emotionally neglected. Poor children are 25 times more likely to suffer maltreatment, 18 times more likely to be sexually abused, and 56 times more likely to be educationally neglected. These effects are due not only to problematic families but also to the neighborhoods in which such children live, the schools they attend, and the peers with whom they associate (Cicchetti & Lynch, 1995).

Peer victimization is a powerful source of maltreatment, and schools are the primary staging areas for this abuse. In the aftermath of school shootings, there is heightened concern about peer bullying. Less publicized is maltreatment from educators, which, according to Hyman and Snook (2001), accounts for 40 percent of the worst school experience reported by students. These researchers identified three types of behavioral problems that are exacerbated by negative school climates:

Hypervigilance. These students have suffered trauma. School climates that help them feel safe counter the view of the world as a dangerous place. Hostile climates keep such students forever on edge and produce "fight or flight" behavior. This is the private logic of these youth: *I felt like I had to watch everybody. I stayed away from the place where it happened. I kept an eye on others so I wouldn't get hurt again. I was afraid to let anyone touch me. I was always waiting for something to happen to me.*

Oppositionality. These students have adversarial relationships with adults in authority. School climates that resolve conflicts respectfully are corrective. Punitive schools and hostile peers justify the logic of defiance. These are examples of the children's private logic: *I picked on other kids. I got angry very fast. I felt like fighting all the time. I hated going to school. I mouthed off to adults. I stopped doing homework. I did whatever I wanted even if people didn't like it.*

Hopelessness. Some students are giving up on life itself. School climates that engage them in positive activities and relationships may offset this self-defeating thinking. When schools are irrelevant and rejecting, hopelessness is exacerbated. Such students think like this: *I felt like a failure. I felt that life was not worthwhile. I don't care about the future. I felt like I would die. I thought about killing myself.*[2]

Alienation develops in environments that tolerate physical and psychological assaults on youth. To be alienated is to feel estranged from others and powerless to change these relationships (Docking, 1990).

Betrayal of Trust

Of all types of maltreatment, violation of children by adults through sexual abuse can create the most lasting trauma. Many experts believe that one million children annually experience sexual abuse, although reported cases are a fraction of that number (Dubner & Motta, 1999). Child sexual abuse is typically defined as an experience between a child and an adult in which the child is subjected to sexual exploitation. Abuse includes fondling and genital contact as well as pornography, prostitution, and exhibitionism. Some professionals believe that abuse may also include overly intimate touching, exposing the child to adult nudity, and making the child bathe or sleep with an older child. Even if the youngster is cooperative, the disparity in power makes any sexual contact exploitative.

Sexual abuse can have long-term negative outcomes on emotional development (Webster, 2002). The degree of damage depends on many factors.[3] Abuse that involves threats, fear, and violence increases trauma. Being molested by a trusted caregiver magnifies the betrayal. Once the abuse becomes known, the reactions of adults are crucial. Sensitive and caring adults calm and reassure the child, whereas those who are accusatory and punitive make the child feel shameful and worthless. If adults refuse to believe a child's report of abuse, the child feels lost and powerless. Individual variables such as temperament, strengths, and social support also affect a child's ability to thrive after abuse. Children abused before adolescence typically show more serious symptoms of trauma than those abused later (Dubner & Motta, 1999).

About two-thirds of sexually abused children are traumatized by this experience, with the rest showing no apparent symptoms. However, a "sleeper effect" can result in increasing behavior problems a year or more after the event. For example, Nathan was abused at age eight by an older cousin but did not show serious effects until adolescence. Then, overwhelmed with homophobic fears, he tried to prove his masculinity by stealing cars with bravado.

Many studies show that childhood sexual abuse can produce symptoms associated with PTSD. These include hyperactivity and agitation; chaotic behavior; reliving abuse in play, drawings, or nightmares; and actual attempts to reenact sexual incidents with peers or adults. The extreme stress suffered by sexual abuse victims can lead to anxiety, depression, conduct disorders, sexualized conduct, ADHD, and confused gender identity. Some escape through truancy and substance abuse. A few are hypercompliant, trying to please and appease adults to gain approval. With this puzzling array of problems, Finkelhor and Browne (1985) suggest that the type of trauma suffered is more important than the particular expression. They identify four varieties of trauma, which we have listed here with parallels to the Circle of Courage:

Betrayal of trust (disrupted belonging). When children have been manipulated and exploited by those who should care for and protect them, trust is the casualty. Children can feel betrayed by caregivers who abuse as well as by those who fail to prevent abuse. When a family refuses to believe a child, or when the child is blamed or ostracized, this contributes to betrayal and broken belongings.

Sexualized socialization (disrupted mastery). Children are traumatically sexualized when their ideas, emotions, and behaviors are shaped in a destructive fashion by sexual abuse. Such children engage in developmentally inappropriate behavior. Having learned to exchange sexuality for affection, such children are confused about love and have severe boundary problems.

Learned helplessness (disrupted independence). Offenders override the victim's will and autonomy, leaving him or her powerless. This occurs both when a child's body has been violated against the child's will and when the child has been seduced through manipulation. Children who are unable to halt the abuse feel helplessly trapped and lack a sense of efficacy and control over their destiny.

Disrespected and devalued (disrupted generosity). Children stigmatized by sexual abuse blame themselves for what has been done to hurt them. Shame and stigma may be associated with rejection or the fear of rejection if their secret is discovered. Feeling worthless, they do not believe they deserve kindness and respect from others, nor do they believe they are capable of contributing to others.

It is important to differentiate normal sex play from sexually reactive behavior. Sex play is generally spontaneous and includes silliness and exhibition or shyness and embarrassment. Children usually desist from these activities when distracted or talked to by caregivers. In contrast, sexually reactive children are anxious, fearful, angry, or intense. Their sexual behavior involves dominance, coercion, threats, and force, and can persist in spite of correction (Araji, 1997).

Sexually aggressive children act out their own abuse in ways that damage self or others (Araji, 1997). Virtually all have had multiple experiences of emotional, physical, and sexual abuse. For these children, sexual behavior becomes a coping mechanism. Aggressive children may use sexuality as a channel for violence. Fire setting in young children, which mainly involves boys, has similarities with sexual aggression. It is secretive, stimulating, and outside the privy of parents.

About half of children who sexually abuse others molest their siblings. Unlike adult pedophiles, who slowly groom victims, most children who molest simply choose victims who are available or vulnerable. Sexually abused children become highly eroticized at an early age. They may be unable to distinguish between affectionate relationships and sexual relationships, and become aroused by routine physical or psychological closeness (Araji, 1997).

Because sexual abuse often begins in the family, intervention must first focus on family relationships. Unfortunately, the caliber of treatment received by sexually reactive children depends less on their needs than on therapist bias. "Victim therapists" are likely to be supportive and relationship oriented, whereas "offender therapists" are apt to be harsher and more confrontational (Araji, 1997). Punitive adult-offender models are sometimes imported into juvenile settings. However, whether children are victims or offenders, they all need interventions that are responsive to their developmental needs (Marquoit & Dobson, 1998; Brendtro & Cunningham, 1999).

Whereas physically abused youngsters are often willing to discuss their mistreatment, secrecy is widespread among sexually abused children. They have extremely high levels of shame unless one can "normalize" the experience by helping them understand that sexual touching and abuse unfortunately happen to lots of kids (Dubner & Motta, 1999). Group counseling with others who have similar backgrounds can lower barriers as youths discover they are not alone in experiencing these problems.

Disclosing specific abuse triggers mandatory reporting to authorities. Thus a youth who does not wish to get family or friends in serious trouble may never disclose. Even a youth who chooses not to be completely open may benefit from indirect discussions of how "some kids" who are abused believe they are bad persons instead of realizing that bad things happened to them. Caring adults who can discuss such problems with a tone of respect help a youth understand that "regardless of what terrible things are in my past, I am worthy and lovable."

MALPRACTICE

Our kids are our most precious asset, and if we do anything less than our utmost to make sure they have a future, then we are failing them.

—Judge William J. Hibbler
(Hibbler & Shahbazian, 1999, p. 150)

Beyond narrow legal definitions, *malpractice* means failure to follow acceptable standards of practice. A fundamental ethic in teaching and healing is to "do no harm." It is a travesty when programs purporting to serve children add to their trauma. In Judge Hibbler's terms, such failures sabotage our children's future.

Most malpractice can be traced to the inability of professionals to create respectful environments and relationships. Research in 10 settings identified common pitfalls and abuses of treatment (Brendtro & Ness, 1982). These include destructive peer climates, depersonalized staff-student relationships, and coercive staff intervention.

Destructive Peer Climates

Distrustful youth seek out antisocial peers to compensate for failure in relationships at home and school. These bonds provide friendships that boost self-esteem but increase children's risk of continuing on pathways of problem behavior. When youth with troubled behavior come together, they can feed one another's problems. Dramatic treatment failures can occur when the informal negative peer culture wields more influence than formal staff interventions (Polsky, 1962; Feldman, 1992).

Antisocial peers often engage in mutual "deviance training" as tough talk reinforces aggressive behavior (Snyder, 2002). Saint Augustine (354–430) described his own deviancy training in a gang of wild youth:

> I would be ashamed to be less vicious than, by their bragging of their wickedness, I understood that they were; for so much the more was their bragging as they were the more beastly. And we delighted in doing ill, not only for the pleasure of the act, but even for a desire of praise. (Augustine, 1923, p. 60)

When operating in groups, individual youths often assume that their peers are more antisocial than is the case (Gold & Osgood, 1992). Thus, if 10 boys march off to a gang fight, most will wish to back down but fear appearing weak to peers. Mistakenly believing that their comrades are fiercely committed to deviance, youth "unwittingly conspire to altercast one another into the delinquent role" (Gold & Osgood, 1992).

An often-cited article in *American Psychologist* argues that peer group treatment is "iatrogenic," that is, that this treatment creates harm (Dishion, McCord, & Poulin, 1999). Such research selectively highlights group treatment failures but ignores successful peer helping programs.[4] The simple reality is that all negative peer cultures are iatrogenic, but sophisticated methods are necessary to turn such cultures around. Some of these strategies are discussed in Chapter 6.

Depersonalized Relationships

Children in conflict have frayed human bonds, and their most potent need is to connect with caring adults. But Peter Benson (1997) reports that 80 percent of adults who encounter youth avert their eyes. This reflexive response sends a powerful nonverbal message: Connection is not welcome.

Many adults do not realize how sensitive a youth may be to cues of liking or rejection. The youth may be scanning the adult carefully, and if a positive response is not forthcoming, this may be interpreted as rejection. The following anecdote illustrates this point:

Luke was an orphaned Native American student being reared by a grandmother. He attended a predominantly white school with an all-white faculty. Teachers recalled problems his older brother had had in a Native American gang several years earlier. When a counselor had gotten to know him, Luke asked why teachers in the school didn't like him. He had been keeping track, and only two staff members had ever greeted him during his time in high school. He explained, "I walk down the hall, and sometimes, out of the side of my eye, I see a teacher looking at me, but when I look back at them, they turn away. I think they are afraid of me."

Most discussions of professional maltreatment steer clear of the problem of racism, although racism is one of the greatest impediments to helping professionals (Rutstein, 2000). Many programs have a double disparity: Children of color are overrepresented, whereas staff of color are underrepresented. Psychologist Jamie Chambers (2000) describes his own sense of pervasive danger when, as an African American adolescent, he was sent to a virtually all-white private school. "I would carry a short bat in my book bag, ever vigilant lest one of the racist students were to speak the terrifying "N" word and I would have to act to defend my dignity" (p. 14).

The most pervasive form of professional malpractice in many settings is the failure to create *cultural safety* for children (Fulcher, 2001). It is not enough for staff to be "colorblind" and "treat all youth the same." The theories of child development used by professionals are often culturally biased and disrespectful. Even simple notions such as "family" and "discipline" have totally different meanings among various cultures. When helpers from a dominant culture ignore these differences, they unwittingly create culturally toxic environments.

The historic distrust accompanying racism can preclude trusting alliances. Helpers have a professional duty to create cultural safety in their personal relationships as well as in the educational or treatment environment. Racism is rooted in beliefs of superiority, whereas cultural safety requires a respectful openness to people of other backgrounds. Racism must be replaced with a belief in the oneness of humankind, a recognition that the only race is the human race (Rutstein, 2000).

Depersonalized behavior management systems create barriers between adults and children. The word *discipline* comes from the root *disciple,* suggesting that powerful learning occurs in close mentoring relationships. But many "discipline systems" substitute rules for relationships; the focus is on meting out depersonalized punishments rather than engaging in genuine teaching or mentoring.

Schools and treatment programs often take shortcuts to teach discipline. Typically this involves prepackaged consequences for undesirable behaviors. Problems are documented by a paper trail with a cursory report of disruptive behavior and the punishment meted out. Although such forms are meant to document behavior and motivate students, they do neither. Depersonalized discipline systems shed virtually no light on what caused the problem and provide youth with no intrinsic motivation to correct the behavior.

Many so-called treatment interventions are little more than lists of graduated sanctions and punishments. Karen Vanderven (2000) demonstrated that rigid point systems make staff feel secure but prevent the tailoring of interventions to student needs. Rule-tethered discipline systems spawn an artificial social culture in which staff and youth communicate in an alien language she calls *pointese:*

> "You'd better shape up or you're going to lose points for that."

> "Tina has earned enough points for level 3 but really belongs at level 1."

> "You can't go on the field trip because you don't have enough points."

Providing behavioral feedback is crucial communication, but sometimes the medium becomes the message. When entire team meetings are spent managing point systems for

rule infractions, prosocial behavioral goals and positive relationships become casualties. Vanderven calls for replacing
groupwide point tallying with individual goal planning in an
alliance between youth and adults.

Although close positive bonds with adults are crucial, the
ratio of staff to youth is not a reliable indicator of the quality
or quantity of attention a youth receives. Rich staffing creates
the potential for close connections, but only if adults are
engaged with youth in respectful interactions. While touring a
20-bed detention facility, we quietly tabulated how many
adults were in contact with the youth. We encountered 15 staff
members on our brief tour, but most were sequestered behind
observation glass or in offices off-limits to youth. Only 2 were
in direct communication with young people. No doubt some
were busy with paperwork, phone calls, or meetings. We fear
that many staff members found face-to-face interactions with
relationship-resistant youth awkward, and so they retreated to
other tasks.

Some adults avoid close relationships with children out of
concern that they might be accused of inappropriate sexual
contact. This is a particular problem in work with sexually
abused children, who need opportunities to experience intimacy in relationships that are not sexualized (Finkelhor &
Williams, 1990). Such children may lack appropriate boundaries and require close supervision. However, a radical "no
touch" policy cuts children off from normal nurturance.

A staff manual in a treatment program for sexually reactive
children illustrates the problem. Adults were not allowed in
youths' rooms for any reason. Students could converse with
staff only at their duty station, and even here they were cued to
keep at least three feet from staff. Also strictly prohibited were
"horseplay, practical jokes, and favoritism." If any youngster
singled out a particular staff member for attention, this triggered immediate staff transfer and an investigation. Elsewhere
the same manual stated that staff should maintain positive
nurturing relationships with students. Adults were in an
impossible bind. A legitimate concern about boundaries had
mutated into barriers to bonding.

Coercive Staff Intervention

It is a formidable challenge to manage difficult behavior without becoming punitive or coercive. Without quality staff training, the most positive treatment program can deteriorate into maltreatment. There is widespread agreement that children in conflict need *structure,* but this word means vastly different things to different professionals (Graham, 1985). In a milieu treatment model, structure involves *cohesiveness,* with staff working in concert to address the needs of children. From a social learning perspective, structure entails *consistency* in behavior management. In the most primitive sense, structure means adult dominance and *coercion.* These very different views of structure are contrasted as follows:

Cohesiveness

> Staff engaged in supportive interactions with children
>
> Youth involved in creating a positive peer culture
>
> High levels of teamwork among staff and with families
>
> Positive bonds maximizing therapeutic interactions

Consistency

> Clearly specified behavioral expectations
>
> Official rules congruent with actual limit setting
>
> Behavioral feedback that is frequent and specific
>
> Consistent rewards following positive behavior

Coercion

> Restricted freedom and invasive surveillance
>
> Adult dominance of activities and rules
>
> Student compliance without choices
>
> Control based on threat of punishment

We are often asked whether boot camps are an effective means of teaching respect to recalcitrant youth. A study reported in *Crime and Delinquency* (Trulson, Triplett, & Snell, 2001) exemplifies this confrontational approach. In Houston, Texas, educators and correctional authorities created the Specialized Treatment and Rehabilitation (STAR) program. Students aged 10 to 16 were referred here for school discipline violations or problems with the court. Their day began at 5:30 a.m. with two and a half hours of regimented military drill and physical activities. Clad in military fatigues and sporting shaved heads, the STAR students were escorted to their regular classes, still in the custody of drill instructors. Two more hours of programming came after school.

Researchers compared STAR students with those given traditional court supervision. A year after boot camp, over half of the STAR students had been re-arrested versus only a third of the comparison group. In spite of poor long-term outcomes, many teachers applauded STAR, apparently pleased to have correctional officers helping enforce school discipline. When students were asked about their experience, 61 percent indicated that "my teachers treat me like an outcast since STAR." Most disagreed with the statements "I would like to be like STAR staff" and "There are staff I can talk to." In general, the students believed they were permanently labeled troublemakers and in the future would probably hang around youth who had been in the boot camp program. In sum, the effect of this boot camp was to stigmatize students, prevent bonding to school and adults, and increase the risk for serious delinquent behavior.

The researchers concluded, "It is important to ask questions regarding what it is we are doing when we seek to control children in schools with police rather than with teachers and principals" (Trulson, Triplett, & Snell, 2001, p. 577). Get-tough, punitive approaches may get good press but do not produce lasting positive changes. Father Val Peter (1999a), director of Girls and Boys Town, is flooded by youth who are casualties of such programs. In his words, "For every kid helped by a boot camp, I can show you ten who got worse" (p. 135).

Unless professionals are solidly grounded in youth development principles, any educational or treatment approach can become coercive. A prominent residential treatment center had a long history of serving challenging children but experienced a crisis of leadership when its longtime director retired. The board appointed an inexperienced successor, and within months, the culture of caring was destroyed. This excerpt from the staff training manual exemplifies the mind-set that justifies coercive controls. Workers were trained to take no crap and to aggressively confront youth using a model called "provocative therapy":

> On a daily basis, residents will try every trick in their repertoire. You don't have to take abuse from the clients just because you are staff. No one pays enough to warrant your poor treatment. It is okay to let clients know you are authority. You should be respected and your directions followed. You will have good days and bad days. Youth can change in a heartbeat, so be prepared at all times. At some point you will probably be slapped, punched, kicked, bitten, scratched, gouged, spat at, have things thrown at you, and have your hair pulled. Additionally, your property may be targeted, such as your car having rocks thrown at it, clothing torn, keys stolen, etc.

Expecting the worst is a self-fulfilling prophecy. Staff strutted their power in front of youth who fought them every step of the way. Staff resigned and students ran away. Parents were outraged and referral agencies withdrew children. Physical restraint and exclusion skyrocketed, as did serious injuries to staff. When the program hit bottom, the board brought in a new administration. Staff were retrained in the strength-based models described in this book, and the program now serves very emotionally challenged children in a stable, safe environment.

"SILENCED AT 14"

Joan's Story

A ninth grader at the time, Joan Braune was appalled to learn about the abuses suffered by many youth who had been sent to boot camps. After hearing about the death of Gina Score at one such state-funded camp, Joan was moved to write this story.

———————

Gina Score was 14, just my age, when she was run to death in a boot camp near my hometown.[5] On her second day in a youth corrections program, she had been forced to run nearly three miles—despite the fact that she weighed 226 pounds and it was a hot and humid day. When she collapsed, the other girls gathered around, trying to provide some shade for the barely conscious teen. They were shooed away by the staff, who yelled, "We're not here to make her comfortable!" Gina died en route to the hospital, after lying on the ground for three hours without medical attention.

Once this story broke, more news of the abuse began to come out, sparking the state into action. Teens told horror tales of being restrained for hours, denied prescribed medications for days, and being forced to eat their own vomit. The Youth Law Center, a national advocacy organization, forced the state into a legal settlement. Gina Score's parents filed a lawsuit against the state. A new organization was founded by parents who wanted to protect their children from abuse by juvenile corrections facilities. Wanting to give a voice to teens who had been mistreated, I founded an organization known as Young Activists for Justice.

With further research, I soon learned that mistreatment is happening all over the country in programs that are supposed to be helping troubled youth. Although Gina Score died in a government-funded boot camp, others don't have to go on trial to be punished and abused in this manner. For thousands of dollars a month, parents can *pay* to send their child to a "behavior modification camp." These camps are located in many remote areas of the United States and in other countries. Behind closed doors, youth are often subjected to brutal abuse, including being harassed by peers, forced to stand without moving for hours, enduring applications of electric shocks, and being doused with pepper spray. Jordan Riak of Parents and Teachers Against Violence in Education maintains a Web site that documents such abuse **(www.NoSpank.net)**. Alexia Parks exposed the inner workings of these settings in her book *An American Gulag: Secret POW Camps for Teens.*

I found that most people don't realize that the United States is the only democracy in the world that has not adopted the Convention on the Rights of the Child—the treaty agreed to by the United Nations that demands fair treatment for youth. As the truth becomes clear, it will shock you, puzzle you, and draw you into the secret world of the "gulag." We need to expose such mistreatment, which is taking a deadly toll on our nation's most needy children and youth. We need to provide these young people, who too often are silenced, with a chance to speak out. Gina didn't have that opportunity.

NOTES

[1] This discussion draws extensively from reviews of research by Cicchetti and Lynch (1995). Dante Cicchetti is a leading researcher on maltreated children who himself experienced this background. He edits the *Developmental Psychopathology* handbooks.

[2] Adapted from Hyman and Snook (2001). Reproduced with permission from the journal *Reclaiming Children and Youth.*

[3] This discussion of sexually abused children draws extensively from Webster (2002).

[4] Many programs described as "positive peer culture" are not accurate exemplars of that method. Often such programs themselves constitute malpractice in that the peer group is empowered to discipline rather than help, resulting in more coercion than concern. Some research further confuses the issue by mislabeling various residential programs that use some group therapy as "positive peer culture" (Chamberlain, Fisher, & Moore, 2002). For research on successful peer helping programs, see Gold and Osgood (1992) and Gibbs, Potter, and Goldstein (1995).

[5] Adapted from Braune, J. (2001). "Children in the American Gulag." *Reclaiming Children and Youth, 10*(2), 81–82. Joan Braune is a youth editor for this journal.

CHAPTER FOUR

The Dance of Disturbance

Dr. Karl Menninger (1893–1990) was a towering figure in American psychiatry for much of the 20th century. A lifelong interest in Native American wisdom influenced his approach to psychiatry.[1] When in his nineties, Dr. Menninger once told us he expected that of all his books, *The Vital Balance* (1963) would have the most enduring impact. That work redefined healthy emotional adjustment as *living in harmony with self and others*. When lives are out of balance, stress, conflict, personality problems, and even self-destruction result.

HARMONY VERSUS DISCORD

Emotional disturbance is not a solo performance but a dance with multiple partners. No matter who takes the lead, others play supporting roles. Nicholas Hobbs, who established the Re-ED model for troubled children, noted that most disturbed behavior results from *discord* in the ecology rather than *disease* in the child (Hobbs, 1994). When a significant person in a child's world can no longer tolerate the tension, the youngster is labeled "emotionally disturbed." A parent or authority declares, "I can't put up with this kid! Something must be done!" Usually this means doing something to the child.

People with *externalizing disorders* act out their problems, creating conflicts in their relationships with others. Those with *internalizing disorders* are anxious and depressed and often cope through withdrawal or self-harm. Schools use such terms as *behavioral disorders* (BD) and *emotional disturbance* (ED) to describe students with troubled behavior, who generally have difficulty establishing satisfactory interpersonal relationships.[2]

James Kauffman (2000) cautions against making too much of the distinction between emotional disturbance and behavioral disorders. One is the inner turmoil, and the other is the outer manifestation of a life in discord.

With each new edition of the *Diagnostic and Statistical Manual* (DSM) of the American Psychiatric Association, the list of "mental disorders" expands (Buetler & Malik, 2002). Hundreds of overlapping labels are now used to describe varieties of problem behaviors. To simplify this maze, the term *disruptive behavior disorders* is used to describe three major patterns of problems (Quay & Hogan, 1999):

Attention deficit hyperactivity disorder (ADHD) includes children who frustrate parents and teachers by their impulsive and distractible behavior.

Oppositional defiant disorder (ODD) is a psychiatric label for young people who engage in adversarial encounters with authority figures.

Conduct disorder (CD) is a diagnosis applied to youngsters who externalize conflict and violate the rights of others.

Ironically, these disorders are defined mainly by the emotions they stir up in adults. Can a youth have a "disruptive behavior disorder" without somebody to disrupt? Does a tree falling in the forest make any sound if no one is there to hear it fall? Kids are called disruptive and disturbed when others in their life space feel disrupted and disturbed. Conflicts in interpersonal relationships are at the center of all major emotional disorders of children (Sroufe, 1990).

Millions of children display disruptive behavior. The *Journal of Child and Adolescent Psychiatry* reported a large study of students in regular classes in three regions of the United States. Teachers rated their students using the diagnostic criteria for the three disruptive behavior disorders (Nolan, Gadow, & Sprafkin, 2001). Here in sum are the results of their ratings for elementary and secondary students:

- Attention Deficit Hyperactivity Disorder (ADHD)—Over 20% of boys and about 8% of girls were identified with symptoms of ADHD.

- Oppositional Defiant Disorder (ODD)—Nearly 7% of boys in elementary school and 5% in secondary school were rated as having ODD. Girls again were lower, at a little more than 2%.

- Conduct Disorder (CD)—About 4% of males qualified for this label, whereas 1% or more of girls were so identified by their teachers.

Many children qualify for more than one diagnosis, which is called *comorbidity.* One bright, creative girl at Allendale boasts 10 DSM diagnoses in her file! Those labels don't tell us as much as knowing that she suffered physical and sexual abuse from her parents and has been bounced from 22 foster homes.

Children exposed to many risks and stressors show a host of negative outcomes. Thus kids with ADHD often display symptoms of anxiety, depression, and conduct disorder as well (Doucette, 2002). There is also a high correlation between substance abuse, delinquency, discipline problems in school, premature sexual activity, and various other risk-taking and rule-breaking behaviors (Donovan, Jesser, & Costa, 1988). How can one make sense out of this jumble of problem labels? Accumulative stress and adversity produce maladaptive coping patterns that are then diagnosed as pathology (Sameroff, 2000).

Researchers from the Oregon Social Learning Center describe how children and caregivers can become involved in coercive interactions (Reid, Patterson, & Snyder, 2002). Frustrated adults revert to punitive and rejecting responses. These patterns can start in the family and continue in later relationships in the school and community. Adults working with youth who show disturbing behavior are easily drawn into counter-aggression. Long (1995) identified situations that put adults at risk of becoming counter-aggressive:

Caught in a conflict cycle. When a youth defies authority and yells, "I am not going to do it!" the normal impulse is to yell back, "Yes you will!" Once the conflict is engaged, the adult has great difficulty backing down.

Personal values and beliefs threatened. Adults may have very different backgrounds from those of the youth they serve.

Bad manners, foul language, and disrespect can be offensive to adults with middle-class value systems.

Being stressed or in a bad mood. Even well-trained adults come unglued when overwhelmed or exhausted. On days when we feel lousy, a youth making humorous armpit sounds can send us into orbit.

Frustration, rejection, and helplessness. We want to do a good job, but when we know we are being ineffective or are treated shabbily, we search for a target on which to displace our fury.

Counter-aggression damages relationships and can lead to physical encounters. A survey of teachers of students with behavior disorders found that 20 percent reported being injured by a student during the previous year. But it may be the adult's own behavior that creates this risk. Those reporting injuries were likely to be males who scored high on a measure of aggressiveness and low on empathy (Center & Calloway, 1999).

Because of the potential destructiveness of counter-aggression, all staff working with challenging youth need specific training in the prevention and de-escalation of crises (Crisis Prevention Institute, 2002). People with professional training are not immune from being drawn into practicing counter-aggressive techniques of verbal confrontation, threats, physical restraint, seclusion, and time out (Wood, 1988). Such methods stir the dance of disturbance. Many adults believe they need to use these aversive interventions to control behavior, but also recognize that punishment does not produce positive growth or lasting change. This contradiction is related to stress and burnout among many who work with children and youth in conflict.

If discord in relationships underlies disturbance, what is the foundation of positive adjustment? Research from diverse traditions points to strengths like those described in the Circle of Courage.[3] A classic study by Stanley Coopersmith (1967) indicated that children build their self-worth upon foundations of significance, competence, power, and virtue. In Circle of

Courage terms, significance is nurtured in communities that foster belonging. Competence develops with opportunity for mastery. Power is widely available only if each person's need for independence is respected. Finally, virtue is reflected in the preeminent value of generosity. Because belonging, mastery, independence, and generosity are precursors to positive development and self-worth, the Circle of Courage might be described as the human resilience code.

THE HUMAN RESILIENCE CODE

Resilience science is the study of human courage. Investigators identify strengths and supports that enable youth to surmount adversity. Some of the leading experts in this field are professionals who themselves overcame difficult childhoods.[4] For a time, researchers sought to profile the so-called invulnerable child (Anthony & Cohler, 1987). As it turns out, no child is invulnerable. Nor is there a profile of the resilient personality.

The picture that is emerging is that resilience is not a rare trait possessed by a few superkids, for most children achieve resilient outcomes. Studies of children adopted from Romanian orphanages found that with new relationships and experiences, most survived earlier severe deprivation (O'Connor, Rutter, & English and Romanian Adoptees Study Team, 2000). Resilience appears to be a normal human capacity to cope with even extreme adversity. All of us are resilient because we are descendants of ancestors who prevailed against every kind of adversity. The proviso is that successful coping requires the cultivation of inner strengths and external supports.

The epic study of resilience by Emily Werner and colleagues followed high-risk children from the Hawaiian island of Kauai from birth to mature adulthood (Werner, Bierman, & French, 1971; Werner & Smith, 1992). They found that the developmental outcome of virtually every risk condition depended on the quality of the rearing environment. Resilient outcomes were associated with close bonds to at least one caregiver, sometimes a person outside of the family. Most resilient youth were not particularly gifted academically but used whatever skills they had to reason and solve problems.

They also developed a sense of personal power and autonomy that enabled them to shed the trappings of problematic backgrounds and take control of their lives. They were likely to find purpose by caring for others, and many relied on spiritual faith that gave meaning to their lives. Although these children had difficulties in childhood and adolescence, early adulthood brought new possibilities for growth. Eventually about 60 percent of the children from any high-risk background made a positive adjustment, though some matured more slowly than others.

Victor Frankl (1984) observed that, throughout most of human history, the precarious struggle for survival has given purpose to life. Once survival is assured, the question becomes, Survival for what? Abraham Maslow (1954) made a similar distinction between *deficit needs* critical to physical well-being and *growth needs* essential to social and emotional health.

Table 4.1 shows that the Circle of Courage is grounded in universal growth needs for attachment, achievement, autonomy, and altruism. As discussed next, these "four A's" have all been shown to be foundations of resilience and positive youth development. But when these most basic growth needs are not met, children display disturbances in development. Belonging, mastery, independence, and generosity turn out to be antidotes to these serious problems.

Attachment versus Alienation

Children are biologically programmed to view other humans as "the most important objects in the world" (Csikszentmihalyi, 1990, p. 164). For optimal development, several concerned adults *beyond the child's immediate family* should support positive growth (Benson, 1997). Children do not form attachments randomly, but selectively connect with people who treat them with sensitivity (Cassidy, 1999).

When they lack opportunities for positive attachments, children experience fear of rejection and abandonment. Initially, children seek coping strategies to restore bonds (Ainsworth, 1989). Psychiatrist Harry Stack Sullivan (1953)

Table 4.1

Resilience Science and the Circle of Courage

Growth Needs	When Needs Are Unmet	Circle of Courage
Attachment	Alienation	Belonging
Achievement	Incompetence	Mastery
Autonomy	Irresponsibility	Independence
Altruism	Selfishness	Generosity

believed that the close relationships of childhood *chumships* could help overcome problems from earlier disturbances in relationships with parents. If substitute attachments cannot be found, the pain of lost self-worth can lead to rage and depression. British researcher John Bowlby (1982) describes two types of anger triggered by abandonment or rejection.

The anger of despair is seen in youth who believe "It's no use. I deserve rejection." These children feel deep shame and worthlessness and see themselves as totally powerless to overcome rejection. They obsess about self-punishment and fantasize revenge against the rejecting adult.

The anger of hope is seen in youth who believe "It's not fair. I don't deserve rejection." They draw on memories of positive attachments and believe they deserve better. Indignant at their treatment, they are more likely to direct anger at others than blame themselves. Most seek "substitute belongings."

Broken belongings are at the epicenter of human suffering. Of the small number of plots in the world's fiction and drama, more than 80 percent are stories of conflict and loss (Pinker, 1997). No human is ever free from the existential crisis of abandonment. Martin Buber translated the Zulu words for "far away" as "where someone cries out 'Oh Mother, I am lost'" (Buber, as cited in Safran & Muran, 2000, p. xi).

Achievement versus Incompetence

All children are motivated to master their environment. Competence is essential for social, academic, and emotional well-being (White, 1959). Many psychologists see the search for competence as the basic motivation for behavior. Lacking opportunities for mastery and achievement, the child experiences confusion and frustration. When confronting a challenging task, a child uses particular coping strategies to solve the problem. If success is not forthcoming, the fear of failure leads to avoidant behavior, as seen in many low-achieving students, or to aggression, as seen in hostility to authority. Because chronic failure leads to devaluation by significant others, it can also trigger the social emotion of shame (Tompkins, 1963b).

Two very different types of achievement motivation have been identified (Nicholls, 1990):

Egoistic motivation is wrapped in the belief "I want to be better than others." Such persons focus more on how they measure up to others than on what they accomplish. Although competition can be a motivator, it can also undermine interest, creativity, and problem-solving ability.

Task motivation is characterized by the mind-set "I want to do my best." The human brain is designed to search for solutions to challenging problems. The focus is on performing the task with skill and efficiency, as opposed to the constant distraction of self-conscious comparison with others.

The quest to inflate test scores to be better than others only fuels egoistic motivation. Even many measures of self-esteem are biased so that positive self-esteem can be scored only if people describe themselves as above average. Nicholls (1990) viewed this as counterfeit competence. He proposed judging people's self-worth by their feelings about the value of what they are accomplishing and the meaningfulness of their work. Most highly talented achievers are driven by a deep interest in their task rather than egoistic competition:

The roots of the word "compete" are the Latin *con petire,*
which meant "to seek together." What each person seeks
is to actualize her potential, and this competition improves

experience only as long as attention is focused primarily on the activity itself. If extrinsic goals—such as beating the opponent, wanting to impress an audience, or obtaining a big professional contract—are what one is concerned about, then competition is likely to become a distraction rather than an incentive. (Csikszentmihalyi, 1990, p. 73)

Autonomy versus Irresponsibility

The desire for freedom and independence is present even in very young children. The quest for self-control increases as children mature. Adolescents who achieve healthy independence generally maintain supportive relationships with parents who honor their autonomy (Hill, 1993). Children not securely attached to adults have great difficulty becoming securely independent. Youth who lack a sense of control over their destiny often display one of two broad patterns of problems (Rothbaum & Weisz, 1989):

Rebellion is seen in youth who believe "Nobody is going to tell me what to do." They assert their power by engaging in purposely defiant behavior, rule breaking, truanting from home, and joining an antisocial or substance-abusing group. These youth may even flaunt their badness because the defiant display is central to their assertion of power (Stott, 1982). Defiance can give youth a false sense of pride based on their ability to project power and coerce others.

Helplessness is the mind-set of youth who feel "What's the use? Nothing I do will make a difference." They also desire control and freedom but believe it is futile to try to assert power and shape their destiny. Youth who lack an "internal locus of control" feel like pawns of others who control their lives. The lack of "self-efficacy" is the belief that one is unable to master challenges in life. Helplessness fuels depression, and those youth are at risk of self-abusing behavior, including retreat into chemicals, eating disorders, and suicide.

Many conflicts between youth and authority figures are related to the desire for freedom and autonomy associated with normal development. However, the protracted period of pre-adulthood in modern culture keeps many young persons from gaining autonomy. The sense of powerlessness is exaggerated in youth who have experienced oppression because of their social or cultural status. Carol Gilligan and colleagues (1991) have shown how girls, in particular those from minority backgrounds, face unique challenges in asserting their power and authority in a society they experience as racist and sexist. If children are to become responsibly independent, they must have a sense of hope (Menninger, 1959) and "self-efficacy" (Bandura, 1977), which springs from the belief that "I am in control of my destiny."

Altruism versus Selfishness

Humans have a predisposition toward empathy and generosity that is present even in infancy. Shortly after birth, babies in a nursery will cry and show distress at the sound of another baby's crying. Remarkably, recordings of their own cries do not produce this effect (Sagi & Hoffman, 1976). As soon as they develop coping skills, children often console other people in distress. A newspaper account described a two-year-old girl who was the only one home when her father was shot and killed in a drug deal. Some time later, when suspicious neighbors entered the silent house, the small girl was still standing guard beside her fallen father. When he got cold, she had covered him with a blanket.

Although the propensity for empathy is inborn, it must be nurtured. When toddlers are exposed to a child in distress, some offer comfort and help; others avoid or even attack the crying child (Radke-Yarrow, Zahn-Waxler, & Chapman, 1984). Whether these differences in empathy result from temperament or training, parents and teachers need to work hard to help all children become sympathetic and show concern for others (Lickona, 2001). Without opportunities to experience generosity, youth cannot develop an authentic sense of self-worth.

Children who lack empathy are self-centered, are exploitative, and show little remorse. They operate on the moral premise that "might makes right." Adults who respond with coercion operate at the lowest level of moral development. A weak conscience should be treated as a developmental delay (Gibbs, 1994). Even violent youthful offenders can develop empathy (Matthews, 1995). As one youth related, "I used to figure nobody cared for me, so why should I care? Now I see I was hurting others just like my father hurt me."

Altruism is the antidote to anger. Becoming involved in helping others reverses the tragedies visited on a person (Masterson, 1981). Hans Selye (1978), the pioneer stress researcher, concluded that acts of love, goodwill, and gratitude offer the best means of transforming reckless self-serving impulses.

OPPORTUNITY VERSUS THREAT

The meaning of troubled behavior is in the eye of the beholder. Human brains have innate "bioprograms" to help make sense of our social world (Bruner, 1990). These developed to ensure survival in interpersonal communities. All of us are "folk psychologists" who diagnose those we meet, forming personal theories about their traits and behavior (Heider, 1958; Bell-Dolan & Anderson, 1999).[5] We are highly attuned to cues of social respect or hostility and develop theories to explain the causes of behavior we encounter.

Novice youth workers often make the mistake of assuming that the defiance of a youth is directed at them personally. When they learn to see the behavior from the child's perspective, they are able to deal with the behavior more constructively. The most important skill in working with students with challenging behavior is empathy, or perspective taking. Adults who are able to empathize can see a very different reality. Those who cannot are left to form judgments based on their own egocentric bias.

Adults without specialized training use naturalistic discipline ranging from a nurturing "green thumb" style to "primitive" coercion and punishment (Morse, Cutler, & Fink, 1964). Our observations are filtered through the lens of our own personal beliefs and values. Although private logic helps us make sense of the world, it is based on naïve theories about behavior (Heider, 1958).

The adult's response to a youth's annoying behavior is highly dependent on private logic. When a person believes that hostility is not deliberate, his or her agitation is not as strong. In a classic study (Zillman & Cantor, 1976), an experimenter rudely provoked subjects and stormed from the room. An accomplice then "explained" that the experimenter's behavior was due to stress from a preliminary doctoral examination. Subjects who reinterpreted the rudeness as unintentional and resulting from other problems did not get angry with the experimenter. However, if anger was allowed to escalate to high intensity, any subsequent explanation was soundly rejected, often with profanity. People who feel justified in their anger become unforgiving and obsessed with retaliation.

Table 4.2 shows how the private logic of a helper can influence the kind of intervention that "makes sense."[6] If a problem presented by a youth is seen as a threat, negative emotions bias the adult's thinking. The adult attributes negative traits to the youth and blames the youth for the problem. Focusing on a youth's contrary traits preps the adult for reactive attack or avoidance. However, if the adult is able to view the behavior as a challenge instead of a threat, this mind-set elicits positive emotions and interventions.[7]

Sometimes faulty private logic about troubled behavior comes from formal theories of behavior. Scott Miller consults with therapists who do not know what to do with impossible cases (whom he calls "therapy veterans"). Therapy failure often results from the theory embraced by therapists. They forget that diagnostic labels and treatment models are not reality but only shorthand attempts to describe reality. His rule of thumb is that a theory is useful only if it helps a particular person improve. But sometimes professionals are so wedded to their psycho-logic that they do not listen with an open "beginner's mind." Each youth has a unique story to tell and must be treated with dignity (Duncan, Hubble, & Miller, 1997).

Adults who label challenging behavior in blaming and demeaning ways are primed to respond in ways that are unlikely to serve the needs of youth. Thus problems that begin in the home can be exacerbated by reactive interventions in

Table 4.2

Adult Private Logic about Challenging Youth

Problems as Opportunity

Private Logic →	Emotions →	Response to Youth
Esteeming	**Interest**	**Empowerment**
The adult views a youth as possessing talent, worth, and potential.	The adult is motivated to engage and invest in this young person.	The adult's goal is to cultivate the youth's strengths and potentials.
Empathizing	**Compassion**	**Encouragement**
The adult views a youth as hurting, unhappy, and having problems coping.	The adult is motivated to understand and befriend this youth in distress.	The adult's goal is to help the youth learn to cope successfully.

Problems as Threat

Private Logic →	Emotions →	Response to Youth
Demeaning	**Disinterest**	**Avoidance**
The adult views the youth as flawed or inferior and unlikely to thrive.	The adult lacks strong motives to engage with and invest in this youth.	The adult's goal is to expend minimal effort in dealing with the youth.
Blaming	**Hostility**	**Antagonism**
The adult views the youth as intentionally disrespectful, defiant, and unmotivated.	The adult lacks empathy and is motivated toward avoidance or attack.	The adult's goal is to overpower, punish, or remove the youth.

the school and community. To become part of the solution, adults must rein in their pessimistic private logic about challenging students. Otherwise, they become participants in the dance of disturbance.

"MY RAGING CHILD"
Deborah's Story

Parents of children in conflict need support from many sources.[8] Although some professionals view parents as important team members, others blame parents and tack on labels such as "dysfunctional." Barbara Huff of the Federation of Families for Children's Mental Health calls for eliminating the adjective *dysfunctional* as a descriptor for families. She adds, "If you need a label, call us overstressed and undersupported." Following is a first-person account of what it is like to parent a child who strikes out in rage at those who want to love her.

Our adopted daughter was sexually and physically abused by her biological mother from birth until she was 5 years old. When she should have been experiencing a loving, happy childhood, she was facing great pain and danger, finding that she could not trust the one person she thought she could. When she first came to live with us, she would wander the house in the middle of the night. She would stand over my bed, staring at me while I slept. It is the most eerie feeling when this happens.

Our daughter's anger and rage have been directed mostly at me. At times she has tried to hurt me by throwing knives, breaking glass, and trying to cut me. A few times she has hit me, causing injury. She steals, lies, and lashes out as if she were a crazed person. Many times we have had to literally sit on her to control her from hurting herself or us. She seems to be more loving and caring toward my husband, thus making me feel left out. In fact, my husband at first believed I was making up all these things she was doing to me. I felt very alone.

Our daughter does not like to hug or cuddle and is not able to develop a genuine relationship. She hates anyone who is in authority over her life. In her mind, she cannot trust anyone for a minute, as this would again open her up to the pain of the abuse. She cannot understand that we would never hurt her in any way. We do not even spank her because, when we first tried, she actually thought it was great; she had the idea that hurting someone physically meant love was being demonstrated.

As a mother of this child, many times I have felt guilty that I was doing something wrong, perhaps not trying hard enough to love her. I kept asking myself, "When can I get the love from her a mother needs?" Several times in our relationship, she has hurt me emotionally so badly that I have had to shut myself off from her. I knew that this was not good for her, but it was the only way to protect myself from hurt and pain. At times I have been drawn into her depression and rage and have tried to act like her.

I have been perceived by many professionals to be angry and uncooperative because all they could see is this perfect little girl and a mother who is in total frustration. Since I have been involved in adoptive parent groups, I have found that it is a very common diagnosis that we are at fault and the child is fine.

In writing about our life with our daughter, I began to think about how other parents whose children are filled with rage must feel. It is a mixture of fear, empathy, sadness, and desperation. You know that your child is obviously in a state of mind that you cannot help. When the damage has already been done, it is hard to undo. All of the love in this world seems unable to shut out your child's memories of abuse and pain. At times, you feel that your efforts go without notice. You find yourself asking, "Is this worth it? How long can I go on living like this?" I understand where the rage comes from. In spite of all that has happened, I love my daughter. Sometimes I can understand how she feels, and sometimes I cannot. It is really not an easy life living with a child with rage from abuse.

As parents, we never know what each day may hold, but we pray and hope that someday all the good we have tried to do will affect our child's life in the positive way it should. In the meantime, we deal with our mixed bag of emotions in therapy, and we seek support from other parents. Each of us says to our self, "I am okay, and I am going to give this my best shot, because my child is worth it."

NOTES

[1] This information comes from personal contacts with Dr. Karl Menninger and his colleagues. After retiring from leadership of the Menninger Clinic, Dr. Menninger and his wife, Jeanne, founded The Villages to provide belonging environments for troubled children. He created considerable controversy by contending that esoteric treatment theories obscure the most basic unmet needs of children. He was active in The Villages well into his nineties. He also journeyed to Washington, D.C., to challenge government policies for dealing with Native American children.

[2] Eli Bower, on the basis of extensive research in California schools, included "an inability to build or maintain satisfactory relationships with peers and teachers" as one of five criteria for identifying emotionally handicapped students (1969, p. 22). Other criteria described emotional blocks to learning, inappropriate behavior or feelings, pervasive unhappiness or depression, and physical symptoms or fears. Since 1975, these "Bower criteria" have been incorporated into the federal government's definition of emotional disturbance. Some school officials attempt to withhold special education services from youth who act out in order to cut costs and manage "socially maladjusted" students as discipline problems. As Bower affirmed, this totally contradicts his original research.

[3] Various research traditions describe dimensions similar to the Circle of Courage as essential to positive youth development. The Teaching-Family model developed at Girls and Boys Town is grounded in *relationships, skills, empowerment,* and *spirituality* (Peter, 1999b). Studies of peer group treatment by the University of Michigan show that effective programs cultivate positive bonds to staff and peers, instill school success, foster autonomy, and provide opportunity for service to others through peer helping and community service (Gold & Osgood, 1992). Research on school success shows four factors related to positive outcomes: *relating, coping, asserting,* and *investing* (Stanley & Purkey, 1994). *Relating* is the level of trust a student has toward others. *Coping* is competence in academic and life skills. *Asserting* is the ability to exercise strength with-

out violating others. *Investing* involves making creative contributions without the need for external rewards. Some researchers use two-factor models, which, in Circle of Courage terms, combine belonging with generosity and mastery with independence. Thus Carl Rogers (1939) saw two classes of needs, *affection* and *accomplishment.* Andrus Angyal (1965) labels these *homonomy* and *autonomy,* and Albert Bandura (1995) describes *personal efficacy* and *collective efficacy.* The Circle of Courage concepts have found wide application in education, treatment, and youth development programs. For example, the Circle of Courage has been used as the basis of a violence prevention curriculum (Kress & Randall, 1998), as a model for inclusion of troubled students (Thousand & Villa, 2000), and as the unifying theme for professional practice with behaviorally disordered students (Kauffman, 2000). In the new democracy of South Africa, Circle of Courage principles formed the basis of government policy in child care and juvenile justice, and in the profession of child and youth care (du Toit, 1997).

[4] Warren Rhodes documents cases of troubled youth who became youth work professionals; he was a delinquent and the first graduate of the Job Corps to receive a Ph.D. (Rhodes & Hoey, 1994). Other noted resilience experts with troubled backgrounds as youth include Waln Brown (1983), John Seita (Seita, Mitchell, & Tobin, 1996), and Dante Cicchetti (Cicchetti & Lynch, 1995).

[5] The concept of folk psychology draws from "attribution theory" research in social and cognitive psychology. We attribute causes to behavior, and positive and negative characteristics to people and events (Bell-Dolan & Anderson, 1999).

[6] These charts are based on research on attribution theory and were developed with grant support from the Augustana Research and Artists fund.

[7] At Allendale, staff receive specific training on how their own private logic affects their actions with youth. "Staff Counter-Response Training" has the goal of helping adults avoid the twin pitfalls of being either overly aggressive or inappropriately indulgent. Information on this training is available by contacting Allendale: **www.allendale4kids.org**.

[8] Babel (1993). Reproduced with permission from the journal *Reclaiming Children and Youth.* Deborah J. Babel is an accountant and has been active with the Federation of Families for Children's Mental Health. This is a national parent support and advocacy organization formed by family members of children with mental

health needs. The federation has chapters throughout the United States and also works to identify problems and solutions to important issues (Huff, 2001). For further information, contact the Federation of Families for Children's Mental Health, 1021 Prince Street, Alexandria, VA 22314-2971.

PART II

Solutions

CHAPTER FIVE

Relationship Beachheads

Two hundred years ago, Johann Pestalozzi described the greatest challenge in work with difficult children as being able to give correction and discipline while convincing youngsters of one's genuine love. In Austria, Anna Freud (1895–1982) and August Aichhorn (1878–1949) worked with "wayward youth" and saw their problems as stemming from unmet needs for love.[1] Some with a more scientific bent did not buy this love talk. John Watson, the founder of behavioral psychology, took a contrary position. He argued that adults should avoid excessive emotional involvement and treat children in a "sensible" way. He gave parents this advice:

> Never hug and kiss them, never let them sit in your lap.
> If you must, kiss them once on the forehead when they
> say goodnight. Shake hands with them in the morning.
> Give them a pat on the head if they have made an
> extraordinary job of a difficult task. (Harris, 1998,
> pp. 84–85)

Watson's notions did not hold up to scientific scrutiny. In parenting, as in therapy and teaching, positive relationships have proven to be the foundation of success. Whatever the treatment or educational model, there is widespread recognition that relationships are a necessary precondition to effective intervention (Gold, 1995; Hubble, Duncan, & Miller, 1999). Trusting bonds provide protective emotional experiences that refute deeply held distrust. But adult-wary children fear what they need most: a bond with a trusted adult.

ADULT-WARY KIDS

People see but they are blind.
Intend compassion, but still unkind.
No one knows the pain I bear.
I return their ghastly stare,
Viewed in contempt by those who succor.

—Australian youth in care

Why do some youth view even well-meaning adults as dangerous and not to be trusted? This attitude of distrust has served them well on numerous occasions to protect against threatening or unpredictable adults, so they approach new adults in the same manner. In the child's private logic, beneath the friendly "front" of the adult is a person who, like others before, is not to be trusted (Trieschman, Whittaker, & Brendtro, 1969). When a child is adult wary or shows extreme rebellion, it is usually a sign that adults have not met the child's basic needs for secure attachment and autonomy (Newman & Newman, 1986). Such children are unlikely to learn from adults, internalize values, or respect authority.

The Distrusting Mind

Trust is not some fuzzy, feel-good notion but is based on hard science. The brain's amygdala is in charge of security screening and carefully checks eyes, face, and physical demeanor. In an instant, a tentative decision is made as to whether this person is friend or foe. The higher brain evaluates additional external cues and taps its data bank of past experiences to determine whether the individual matches the profile for safe or unsafe persons: Does the person seem friendly, fearful, or hostile? Am I safe from predatory attack? Am I being treated respectfully? Does this person seem to trust and like me? If the person acts friendly, is this genuine, or could there be an ulterior motive? Does this person respect my race or culture? Is this the kind of person who would be fun to know, who would be willing to help me, who might teach me interesting things?

The most powerful social signals among both humans and animals are those communicated by the eyes. The amygdala can detect at considerable distance if a predator makes eye contact. This once had survival value when one encountered dangerous strangers or carnivores. In a city full of strangers, it can send a false warning. Street-wise youth often justify their aggression by claiming that their antagonist "kept looking at me and disrespecting me." Whether eye contact triggers positive or negative emotions depends on trust or distrust, as the following example illustrates:

> Marcus had been repeatedly sexually molested as a small boy and was extremely distrustful of adults. We first spoke with him when he was locked in a county jail. Whenever guards walked by his cell, he eyed them warily through a wire-glass window. As each passed, he would remark either "I can take that one" or "I can't take that one." In a dangerous world, one must constantly scan for predators or prey (Goleman, 1995). The slightest sign of threat activated his amygdala for an attack or retreat response. Marcus later explained, "I never fight adults who are friendly, just those who look angry or afraid."

Youth may have many reasons for keeping their distance from helping adults (Goldstein, 2001). They may not be attracted to the adult, may fear disclosing painful events, may need to assert power to avoid being controlled, or may retreat in hopelessness. Youth who keep adults at bay are often slapped with labels such as "manipulative" or "resistant." This casts blame on the youth while excusing adult failures to connect. Much adult avoidance is not pathological but is a predictable response to improper procedures, as seen in the following example:

> Charles was sent into detention after attacking a counselor. He reported that the counselor tried to force him to talk about sexual abuse. When he resisted, Charles was told, "If you don't deal with this, you may become a rapist someday yourself." The counselor's motivation to get him to deal with this issue is understandable, but as Charles said, "I want to take my time. I'll come out with it eventually, but I won't be forced to talk."

Youth who expect hostility and rejection operate at heightened levels of alert. They react with strong negative emotions if they interpret an adult's behavior as disrespectful, blaming, belittling, mocking, or shaming. Unwanted affection can also backfire, and distrustful youth feel threatened if they think that somebody is trying to get too close and to discover what they are thinking. This fear of transparency makes them very guarded when professionals try to diagnose their problems. One boy described how hard it is to trust adults who are trying to help:

> I feel like they are starting to seep into the tiny cracks in the armor I've enclosed myself in. If they do, it could be devastation. They would see all the secrets that I've kept away from them for so long. This protective cover that I use is my life support. If they were to crack or puncture it, all of us would surely be hurt.

All humans have some natural wariness of allowing others to get too close. This includes people who are overtly hostile, but also those who seek to establish closeness without the prerequisite rituals of acquaintance. We have an instinctual fear of unwanted intimacy, or *forced teaming* (de Becker, 1998). This offers protection against cunning people who seduce others into letting their guard down as a precursor to exploitation. Jonathan, who spent his adolescence in out-of-home care, offered this advice to those working with distrustful youth:

> You have to let kids connect with you, not try to force it. When people I don't know start asking me personal questions, I think, "I don't even f—ng know you and I'm not telling you s—t." You need to first build bonds and then they will tell you when they feel they are ready.

Building bonds usually requires adult initiative. But people who come on too fast drive youth away. Thus it is helpful to initiate a series of very brief, good-natured interactions in which the adult backs off before the youth becomes uncomfortable. This strategy demonstrates adult interest but avoids triggering escape behavior. Humor and nonverbal warmth also send signals that this adult is friendly, safe, and perhaps even intriguing. Because social interest is a powerful, built-in motivator, friendliness, in time, will override fears of affiliation. When a team of adults is providing relationship opportunities, the young person is even more likely to form an attachment that will thrive.

Fight, Flight, Fool

Children alienated from adults develop sophisticated strategies for blocking adult attempts to provide help or try to change them. They believe their past coping behavior will better serve them than the treatment alternatives we propose, or they believe their situation is hopeless (Wood, 1995). Kids who outwit adults use one of three patterns of defensive behavior: fight, flight, or fool. Following are examples drawn from clinical work with challenging children (Roberts & Jurren, 1968; Seita & Brendtro, 2002).

Fight

I will attack others before they hurt me. Youth with this defensive strategy have had some success controlling adults through power and coercion. At the verbal level, their defiance may operate in a range from disrespectful tone, sarcasm, profanity, and verbal insults to veiled or direct threats. At the physical level, they may use a hostile demeanor, threatening gestures, or direct aggression. Although adults do not want to escalate this anger, such youngsters need a firm response from authority figures who are unflappable. A different pattern is represented by a terrified child whose belligerence to adults is tinged with genuine fear. Thus a child who has experienced maltreatment may say, "Go ahead, beat me. See if I care." Whatever the cause of hostility, children need to know that adults are in charge and will not be provoked into counter-aggression.

Flight

I won't let others get close enough to hurt me. This coping pattern is common among children who are frightened or ashamed. In the normal course of events, they avoid adults, avert eye contact, and may be afraid of physical expressions of warmth. Young children forced to talk to an adult may withdraw, curl up in a fetal position, feign sleep, cover their face and ears, and become mute. Some cry or scream with genuine panic. Children showing retreat behavior may be experiencing guilt or shame and are afraid of being embarrassed or humiliated. Even though their behavior may be inappropriate, these children need reassurance and support. These problems can be solved without scolding and rejecting. Although the adult needs to avoid invading their space, the goal is to stay in communication with the child and convey a sense of safety.

Fool

I won't let others know what I really think and feel. Children with this attitude use techniques to outmaneuver the adult. A youth who has been "in the system" often fears that the adult is trying to "mess with my mind." Such youth develop sophisticated strategies to outwit adults, such as telling them what they want to hear or inventing pseudo-problems to lead them down a false trail. Some act contrite, feign penitence, and offer quick promises of better behavior. They may have been successful at generating lenient, forgive-and-forget feelings in adults and thus avoid having to accept responsibility for their behavior. A problem with younger children is silly or crazy behavior. Attempts to discuss problems may be met with laughing, giggling, animal sounds, or bizarre behavior. In the past, this has exasperated adults, who gave up efforts to communicate. Instead of being upset by this "manipulation," it is better to remain engaged in a serious but nonthreatening manner.

There is no list of management techniques to parry every resistant behavior a youth can contrive. But adults should never get into a tit-for-tat reactive mode by matching youth manipulation with adult counter-manipulation. Distrustful children often test out the adult to see if the person is safe, strong, and worthy of trust. Once trust arrives, most of these behaviors will depart.

Yearning to Trust

Children who are guarded and adult wary are inhibiting powerful inborn needs for attachment. Distrustful children need adults who engage in conscious efforts to build bonds, even if the youth initially tries to push them away. This is not some complex strategy, but involves communicating kindness and respect to youth who are accustomed to seeing adults as the dangerous enemy. As one such youth said, "It's kind of like a cat who has been abused. You can't just go up and pet it."

The patient, step-by-step process by which avoidance becomes approach is seen in the following account of an adult-wary girl. Staff members from an alternative school near Chicago attended the Black Hills Seminars on Reclaiming Youth in South Dakota. They brought with them a 16-year-old student from their school. Initially she appeared very guarded on this strange turf, retreating behind dark glasses and street-tough demeanor. As conference host, the first author welcomed her and learned that her name was Amber.

Over the next two days, I made a point of greeting Amber by name whenever we met. She made only perfunctory responses and hurried on to avoid further conversation. Still, Amber seemed to be interested in the presentations about youth at risk. A young female college student whose sister and niece both had died from AIDS led one session. Afterward, Amber sought out the college student for conversation.

On the third day, Amber approached me before the evening banquet and said, "I just want you to know I respect what you people are trying to do for youth." I thanked her, but the scheduled event prevented further communication.

The following morning Amber was back: "I see a lot of other kids are on the program. I wrote this poem, but I don't want to read it. But I don't mind if you have somebody else read it." I thanked her warmly and promised to have it read.

The next day Amber was in approach mode again: "I changed my mind. If you want me to read the poem myself, I will." Her poem was a big hit, and by conference's end she was relaxed and seemed to enjoy reaching out both to adults and to peers. Her initially guarded and aloof behavior concealed a person who feels deeply and craves love. Her poem follows:

Tears: A Sign of Yearning
by Amber

Tears are falling from a face with no expression. Tears are cried by an empty head. Tears are being shed by a vacant mind. Tears are let loose like a running faucet. With no expressions and no words, we know what those tears are. An empty soul looking to be fulfilled. A broken heart waiting to be fixed. Tears that are covered up, waiting to be revealed. A cry for help, a sign for love. Tears, a sign of yearning.

RANCOR TO RESPECT

Youth who act as if they couldn't care less what adults think are in reality often highly sensitive to criticism. Swiss reeducator Paul Diel (1987) observed that youth realize they have faults, but a tone of *rancor* renders ineffective any attempt at correction. Rancor is an emotionally charged communication that conveys bitterness and malice. Diel saw rancor as the prime symptom of discord in any relationship between children and adults. His first step in work with families or teachers was to try to secure an agreement from the adult that any tone of rancor and reproach would immediately cease.

> We spoke with Tommy, an oppositional fourth grader who repeatedly was sent to in-school detention. He said the teacher is required to give a warning before sending him from the room. "But every morning this week she meets me at the door to her room and says, 'Tommy, this is your first warning,' before I even get to class." He added, "I can tell by the meanness in her voice that she doesn't want me in her class."

Rancor is the polar opposite of empathy and conveys malevolence instead of benevolence. Rancor can be highly subtle, such as a sarcastic inflection. Adults may not be aware that they are sending emotionally threatening stimuli that can trigger an amygdala alarm. Very young children can perceive rancor in language even if they do not understand the words. Rancor can be detected in any language. In American Sign Language, rancor is communicated by facial expression and an exclamatory style of signing. A teacher was having a conference with a boy and his mother, who was hearing impaired. The son was interpreting the meeting for his mother as necessary. At one point the mother became frustrated at him and signed furiously. He responded in sign and word, "You don't have to *shout* at me, Mother!"

The rancor and reproach that mark discord in past relationships must be replaced with empathy. Therapeutic alliances require mutual respect, caring, and understanding. A major barrier to respectful alliances is tension in the interpersonal bond (Safran, Crocker, McMain, & Murray, 1990). Adults who rely on carping and belittling or who ignore and neglect youth will wreck the alliance (Henry, Schacht, & Strupp, 1986).

Another major cause of conflict is disagreement on tasks and goals (Safran, Crocker, McMain, & Murray, 1990). The most straightforward remedy is to enlist youth in setting goals. A student was referred to an alternative school after a long pattern of conflicts with authority. The principal chose to employ a fresh approach: "I looked through your file and it seems that nobody has asked *you* what difficulties you are facing and what you want to happen. Let's start there."

Whether to confront or de-escalate problem behavior is a careful balancing act. Youth who are comfortable with hurting behavior must be challenged, but frontal attacks will only further activate their defensive behavior. Self-centered, narcissistic youth appear not to care what adults think. In reality, they use high-powered microscopes to monitor adult empathy. They are extremely wary, and the slightest insult can lead to disappointment and rage, destroying any wisps of trust that may have begun to form (Masterson, 1981).

Children who distrust adults may have stronger motives for resisting relationships than adults have for building them. The rabbit running for its life has a greater incentive than the fox who is just out for the run (LeDoux, 1996). Adults must keep a respectful posture, even when respect is not immediately reciprocated.

Communicating with Guarded Kids

By nature, children are curious, trusting, and inclined toward social interaction. But children who have been hurt or rejected by adults develop an acute sensitivity to subtle cues that it may happen again. At the extreme, the suspicion that others are enemies is paranoia.[2]

We all have had occasion to believe that others are talking about us behind our back. But our distrust is controlled by reality. Chronic suspicion of others can be dominated by two main fears (MacKinnon & Michaels, 1971):

> *The fear of being harmed.* People believe others wish them ill and are trying to manipulate, exploit, or deceive them. They attribute malevolence to others.

> *The fear of being ignored or discounted.* People believe others disregard their feelings, and they fear rejection or abandonment.

People with such views may totally retreat from interaction, angrily attack, or try to control others. Paranoid people have a pattern of blaming others for their own distress. Although alleged grievances may be fabricated in the person's mind, one should assume that there is at least some sliver of truth that justifies the person's suspicions. Thus it is better to validate these feelings rather than disregard them. The adult who discounts a youngster's suspicions reinforces the child's worldview that "everybody is against me":

Youth: My teacher treated me very unfairly yesterday. She jumped all over me for something somebody else did. I hate her.

Adult: I find it hard to believe that you were punished for nothing. You must have done something to deserve what happened.

Because our adult viewpoint seems so much more logical, we may be unaware that we are ignoring a young person's private logic and feelings. We then come across as moralistic and superior:

Youth: *(raising her voice)* I wasn't provoking anyone. I can't stand the girls in my group. They are always picking on me. I'm going to get them back.

Adult: You have a terrible attitude. Until you start accepting responsibility for your behavior, nobody's going to take you seriously.

We want youth to shoulder responsibility for their behavior, but we will not convey this point if we brush off their perceptions and feelings. When the listener searches for the grain of truth in the person's concern, the youth feels validated. Thus, if a youth claims that peers are talking about her behind her back, initially it is better to join with that thinking than to disregard it: "Well, I know what it must feel like to believe that others are making fun of you." The goal is to acknowledge feelings without exaggerating the grain of truth. Here are some examples of respectful communications that join with the youth:

> **Youth:** My teacher is treating me unfairly. Yesterday he jumped all over me for something somebody else did.

> **Adult:** It sounds like you think the teacher is blaming everything on you and didn't see what the other kid did.

> **Youth:** Yeah, the other kid was in my face, so I called him a name and then pushed him.

> **Adult:** So you got angry when he got in your face, and you started a fight and got in trouble. Do you think it was worth letting him get you so upset?

The goal is not to leave youngsters to wallow in distrust but to gently pull them away from a mentality of distrust toward one of trust and constructive problem solving.

Passing the Trust Test

Trust is often built in a patient, step-by-step process. Many youths follow a predictable two-part strategy to "diagnose" the adult and decide whether or not they trust the adult and want to engage in a relationship (Trieschman, Whittaker, & Brendtro, 1969). Following are the two key strategies youth employ.

Strategy 1: Casing

A youth engages in "orienting behavior" in an attempt to gather information about an unfamiliar situation or person. This involves intense observation by a hypervigilant youth of the subtle behaviors of the adult. If verbal and nonverbal behavior are consistent, the youth knows how to "read" the adult and begins to relax. But any discrepancy (as when the adult's words are friendly but actions are awkward and uncomfortable) can trigger tension in the youth. Youth are highly cognizant of actions that suggest superiority, hostility, insincerity, disinterest, or deception. If these are noted (or mistakenly attributed to the adult), negative emotional responses in the youth cause heightened distrust. Thus an adult who feels the need to come on "tough" out of fear of not being able to control a youth inadvertently builds animosity instead of trust. Youth also are very observant as to how other youth act toward a particular adult. They may show very few problems during this "honeymoon" period.

Strategy 2: Limit Testing

Because one can learn only so much by watching, youth gather more intelligence by actively probing. They seek to learn about an adult from peers. They need to establish how much power and status the adult has. They may directly ask, "What would you do if . . . ?" questions. Ultimately, most youth need some "testy" encounter with the adult to determine whether this person is dangerous, easily manipulated, or a reliable authority figure. If they start to develop some interest or trust in the adult, they need to know whether this person will still be friendly if they show their real problems. Some youth set up specific encounters to test an adult's sincerity. Scott Larson (Larson & Brendtro, 2000) tells of a mentor who was to spend Saturday mornings with a youth who had returned home from a residential placement. For seven weeks, he went to the boy's home, only to find nobody there. Finally, as he walked away in total frustration, resolving not to return, the youth called out from an upstairs window, "Sir, I'm here." In fact, the boy had been there every time. He was patiently testing whether this new adult was worthy of trust.

By casing and limit testing, the youth forms a predictable picture of the adult and knows how to deal with this person. The youth diminishes orienting behavior once having settled on a view of the adult that is negative, positive, or indifferent.

This state of affairs is likely to remain stable unless some significant new experience causes the youth to question his or her initial appraisal of the adult. This is why a crisis poses both opportunity and threat for changing the dynamics of a relationship.

In their eagerness to build relationships, some adults blur the boundaries that enable youth to develop sincere trust. Pursuing a guarded youth too assertively only drives the young person away. Adults who so need to be liked that they act "like one of the kids" become overaged peers, not respected mentors. Adults should never seek to build themselves up by criticizing other adults or the youth's parents. Also, if a youth forms strong ties to the adult, the adult should not promise more than he or she can deliver; the adult is not the youth's new parent.

Once a helping alliance is formed, it is still vulnerable to ruptures. Whatever the cause, adults bear the primary responsibility for weathering this crisis and restoring the bond. A helping adult who acknowledges contributing to the misunderstanding in a caring and nonjudgmental way will provide a totally new experience for many youths. Ruptures in relationships are not signs of pathology but speed bumps on the road of resilience.

TRUST-BUILDING STRATEGIES

Children who have been emotionally wounded harbor what Erik Erikson (1963) called a "basic mistrust" that confounds attempts to help a young person. The opposite of a trusting, respectful alliance is the adversarial encounter. An adult seeking control is pitted against a youth trying to avoid being controlled. Adversarial encounters are power struggles, and nobody likes being coerced. Youth despise dictatorial adults, and adults harbor hostility toward youth who resist being controlled.

In contrast, the helping alliance involves trust, hope, rapport, liking, and mutual respect. The youth feels understood and valued. There is consensus about the tasks and goals as youth and adult join as partners in problem solving (Hubble, Duncan, & Miller, 1999). It is hard for adults and youth to hate or be hated when they join up and struggle side by side to meet important life challenges. Half a century of research has shown that a positive relationship is the single best predictor of treatment success (Hubble, Duncan, & Miller, 1999). Similar findings apply to teachers of students at risk (Gold, 1995). Trusting bonds provide corrective emotional experiences.

Adult-wary youth do not leap into our therapeutic laps. Building relationship beachheads requires purposeful interventions to diminish antagonism and increase the attractiveness of the adult. Youth professionals follow a sequence of strategies for relating to reluctant youth.

Strategy 1: Locate Areas of Commonality

The first order of business when strangers meet is to discover what they have in common. More than casual small talk, this is a bonding ritual. In effect, humans search for an answer to the question "How are we related?" Finding some common interest lowers the stranger barrier. ("Your older sister was in my class a few years ago. How is she doing?") The goal of locating common areas is to turn aliens into relatives in the broadest sense of the word. An orphaned boy who was seeking an adoptive family told his social worker, "See if you can find somebody who knew my mother who might want to adopt me" (Lewis, 2002).

Strategy 2: Initiate Positive Interaction

Positive interaction can include interesting conversation, rewarding activities, and pursuing children's interests. Some youth are incredulous that a grown-up is actually interested in their point of view and enjoys their company. Positive interaction has reciprocal effects, in which both parties become more closely bonded. A boy who was named Ali, after former world heavyweight boxing champion Muhammad Ali, wanted to take boxing lessons, but staff in his group treatment setting resisted because of his past violence. Boxing became the topic of debate between Ali and his grandfatherly therapist, Tom. In time, Tom helped Ali fulfill his dream, and he came to Ali's first match with video recorder in hand. Later, as they watched the tape, Ali shared early trauma that had terrified him for years.

Lacking some major turning point, trust often must be painstakingly built in small, incremental steps. The adult reaches out to a youth with small signs of kindness and then backs off a bit to avoid crowding the youth. In contrast to the conflict cycle, this sets in motion a cycle of warmth and goodwill.

Strategy 3: Provide Support in Periods of Crisis

Children who typically are well defended may be reachable in times of grief, loss, or frustration, or when ill or hurt. When the adult walks through the storms of life with a young person and shares this time of distress, bonding and attachment are enhanced. A teacher attended an evening memorial service for the father of one of his students. The father had been abusive and an alcoholic; he died in a car crash. Very few people were in attendance, and this gesture reversed a previously hostile relationship between teacher and student. It also showed that, because stressful events are imprinted in emotional memory, even minor acts of respect and kindness in these times of arousal are magnified in significance.

Strategy 4: Help Children Develop Strengths

Children do not bond to adults indiscriminately. They are genetically programmed to attach to adults who help them develop strengths and meet their needs. The Circle of Courage targets the core growth needs of belonging, mastery, independence, and generosity. Adults who help children thrive in these areas become significant people in their lives. Following are some descriptors youth use to describe adults they can trust.

Belonging: This adult accepts me, pays attention, listens, jokes with me, really likes me, treats me like he would treat his own kid.

Mastery: This adult understands me, knows what is going on, can talk with me, isn't easily fooled, can help figure out hard problems.

Independence: This adult respects my opinion, doesn't treat me like a little kid, is not afraid of me, has hope for me, doesn't give up on me.

Generosity: This adult is kind and not mean, won't lie, never holds grudges, wants the best for me, would never hurt me.

Strategy 5: Generalize Trusting Behavior

Once a distrustful youth finds the courage to trust a particular adult, the next order of business is to extend attachments to others. A common error among adults is to hog the helping relationship. This is understandable; connecting with adult-wary kids is a formidable victory. The alliance gives the adult legitimacy in recruiting other caring adults. Otherwise, a youth may expect this solo relationship to become a long-term bond.

There is growing recognition of the importance for all youth of finding lifelong connections. It is a huge handicap to have to go through life without what John Seita calls "family privilege." Even older teens without families are being encouraged to consider adoption (Lewis, 2002). Although a youth may have negative feelings about adoption, just being asked to entertain the possibility challenges deeply felt beliefs that "nobody wants me." One older teen was preparing to be adopted by a middle-aged couple, when the husband developed terminal cancer. The adoption proceeded as scheduled. Every day spent with a loving father would give this boy a father to remember for life.

Strategy 6: Celebrate Connections

Once an alliance is established, it needs to be acknowledged and even celebrated with "claiming behaviors" (Fahlberg, 1991). Rituals, nicknames, high fives, humor, and verbal repartee mark and maintain bonds. Claiming behaviors repeat the unspoken message that "we belong to one another." Parents regularly use claiming communications with their own children, including terms of endearment, nicknames, shared humor, and family traditions. Such interactions convey emotions of interest and affection and strengthen connections. A moving example of communicating belonging is found in *Cider House Rules,* the story of a 1940s-era orphanage (Irving, 1985; Halstrom, & Gladstein,

1999). Dr. Larch, the kindly old superintendent, builds close ties with his brood of cast-off kids. Each night, he turns out the lights in the dormitory with this bedtime ritual:

"Good night, you princes of Maine, you kings of New England!"

After Dr. Larch leaves, one young boy, Fuzzy, asks his peers, "Why does Dr. Larch say that every night?"

Curly responds, "Maybe to scare us?"

Another youth corrects him: "No, Dr. Larch loves us."

Fuzzy asks again, "But why does he do this?"

Buster responds, "He does it because we like it."

Fuzzy asks, "Do you like it, Curly?"

Curly responds, "Yeah."

Fuzzy says, "I like it, too."

"JOIN-UP"

Monty's Story

Humans and higher animals are endowed with elaborate brain-based programs for deciding whether to approach or avoid other living creatures. Both craving and fearing contact, we search for clues about all who cross our paths to predict whether this new encounter poses danger or opportunity. Monty Roberts (2001) is probably the world's best-known expert in replacing distrust with trust in a process he calls Join-Up®. He specializes in cases in which prior experience has caused such fear of humans that any contact triggers wild "flight or fight" behavior. Perhaps you have guessed—Monty Roberts is an equine psychologist.

We are indebted to Darrell, who has struggled with PTSD, for introducing us to the career of Monty Roberts, whose work teaching horses to trust humans inspired the popular film *The Horse Whisperer*. When Darrell brought us a book by Monty Roberts, he said, "People call horses 'wild,' but actually they are very smart and know humans are predators. It's that same way with me. When my PTSD kicks in, I get confused and sometimes I see people as predators."

Training horses is a potentially dangerous business. Ordinarily a horse is a flight animal, but if cornered, it can strike out with deadly fury. Monty Roberts is now past normal retirement age and has been training horses since he was a boy. Monty grew up on a California ranch, where his father captured and broke wild mustangs. Monty felt sorry for the horses and believed there must be a better way. At age 12, Monty set the goal of training a wild mustang without hurting it.

On long summer days, Monty would lie on the prairie, peering through binoculars to discover how horses communicate with one another. He was particularly interested in how mares raised their colts. He learned that Native Americans had very different ways of training horses than Europeans. They recognized that horses are curious, social animals who will approach humans if fear can be overcome. Monty learned the language of horses and succeeded at training his first mustang. When he proudly showed his horse to his father, he was punished and warned that these are dangerous animals that can be controlled only through fear.

Monty Roberts has learned how to read the cues horses give when they believe they are in danger. Understanding these signals, Roberts can transform himself from a presumed predator to an object of trust in a short period of time. Recently we had the opportunity to meet Monty and observe him "gentle" several wild horses. He has performed such demonstrations thousands of times, including a presentation before Queen Elizabeth. The following is what we observed.

Hundreds of people filled an indoor arena in the Black Hills of South Dakota to see Monty Roberts in action. They sat in bleachers around a high-fenced circular corral. A local rancher was handed a microphone and asked to describe the first horse being led into the corral with Monty. "This is my gelding, and he has never been ridden—won't even let anybody touch him," the owner announced to the audience. Monty had never worked with the horse before.

The large, dark animal was now fenced with Monty, surrounded by an arena full of humans. Monty stood relaxed in the center of the ring, appearing to ignore the horse. He spoke to the crowd in a calm voice that was amplified by a microphone in his cowboy hat so all could hear. Penned in, the horse knew that it could not escape from Monty or the crowd that surrounded him, and its eyes bulged in terror. In technical terms, the horse's brain was in a state of amygdala alarm.

"We have a very paranoid horse here," said Monty. "I don't want anybody in the bleachers to get up or move or make a sound. If this horse attends to any of you, he will not be paying attention to me, and that could be dangerous."

The horse stood frozen, uncertain of where the greatest danger might lie. Monty explained that he was going to get the horse's attention by taking the stance of a predator. He would face the horse, make piercing eye contact, and hold out his arms with open fingers like the claws of a bear. The horse relied on 50 million years of brain genetics to direct its ensuing actions.

The moment Monty became "the bear," the horse panicked and set off in flight. Of course, the horse was penned, so it ran in a confined circular pathway. Monty stayed in the center of the ring. He explained that the horse would run only the equivalent of a quarter of a mile, and if the horse had not eluded the presumed predator by then, it would need to try new coping methods. A horse that kept fleeing would only exhaust itself or run into new danger.

Monty predicted the behaviors we would see when the horse determined that flight was futile. First, the horse would shift its attention to Monty by training one ear on him. Second, the horse would bare its teeth in a "grass chewing" gesture to suggest that its only intent was to share the same pasture. Third, as the horse continued circling the pen, it would lower its head as if to suggest, "I am willing to renegotiate and let you be in charge." Monty seemed to know what the horse would do before it happened. As if on cue, all three signals were sent. Now, Monty would answer these messages.

Monty dropped his bear-like pose, broke eye contact, and turned at 45 degrees to the horse. The horse immediately stopped and turned with curiosity toward Monty. As the horse warily approached, Monty spoke quietly while slowly rotating 360 degrees, turning his back to the horse briefly, thus establishing that he was not a predator. The horse approached Monty and allowed him to stroke its neck and groom him. "This is the moment of Join-Up," Monty explained. "Join-Up is the single most important step in teaching because it makes all that follows possible."

Monty then put a bridle on the horse and led it around the circle. Next came a blanket over its back, and finally a saddle. Throughout, Monty's gentle talking and stroking reassured the horse. Then he strapped a dummy rider onto the saddle and let the horse buck a bit to discover that the object would not go away but also would cause no harm.

Monty was now ready to teach the horse to trust another human. He beckoned a rider from his staff to enter the ring. The young man was dressed in jeans and a shirt the same color that Monty wore. One might expect that the horse would respond in terror again, but now the horse took its cue from Monty. Monty was not afraid of the new person, so neither was the horse. After allotting a brief period for the young cowboy to join up with the horse as well, the rider mounted and rode the horse. As the rider dismounted and left the pen, Monty checked his watch and announced, "Thirty-seven minutes. I'm sorry it took seven minutes longer than planned, but this was a very hyperactive horse."

In a final demonstration of the power of Join-Up, Monty positioned himself across the ring from the horse. He reminded us that half an hour earlier, the horse had seen him as a predator. Monty told us in the audience that we were to begin clapping on his signal, and the instant he signaled us to stop, we must all be silent again. Monty's hand rose and cued us to applaud. The burst of noise filling the arena terrified the horse, but this time it did not set off in blind flight. The horse now knew just where to go—straight across the ring to the safety of Monty, who then waved us into silence. The horse had found protection from its previous predator. The audience was in awe.

Monty's latest book is called *Horse Sense for People*. He is now doing his demonstration at prisons, at conferences, and for charities that use horses in therapeutic programs for children. He explains that his work is not just about gentling horses but about reteaching humans how all creatures were meant to live together. For thousands of years humans have tried to control animals—and one another—with the principle "Do what I say or I will hurt you." There is a better way, and Monty is teaching this to executives, educators, parents, and of course, horse trainers.

Monty reports that often at the end of a program, some people linger to share personal experiences. A typical example is a husband and wife in tears, having recognized the destructive relationships they have been acting out with one another and with their children. The old cowboy listens to their story, recalling his own discovery as a young boy that kindness is more powerful than coercion.

NOTES

[1] August Aichhorn and Anna Freud trained Fritz Redl, who emigrated from Austria to the United States at the beginning of World War II. Redl applied these ideas to work with aggressive children, as described in the classic book *Children Who Hate* (Redl & Wineman, 1951).

[2] This discussion is drawn from a presentation by Dr. Pat Taglione at the Allendale Association, Lake Villa, Illinois, September 2000.

CHAPTER SIX
Cultivating Strengths

In the 19th century, Goethe declared that the job of the educator was to find the germ of virtue concealed in the kernel of every fault. The 20th century was heralded as "the Century of the Child," when science would point the way to new solutions to long-standing problems of young people (Key, 1909). But as helping disciplines became hyperspecialized and programs became depersonalized, there was a loss of vision and hope. Professionals lost sight of the potentials of young people and became preoccupied with deviance, deficit, and disorder. Karl Menninger was an early critic of pessimistic professional mind-sets preoccupied with pathology instead of health:

> We have always taught psychiatry wrongly as I view it;
> we've approached it from the back end. . . . It is as if a
> surgeon would hand out a platter of bloody fragments of
> human tissue to ignorant laymen and say "this is the
> result of surgery." (Menninger, 1988, pp. 95–96)

Maria Montessori (1948) challenged educators who failed to see promise in disadvantaged children. She interpreted the resistance of defiant children as courage and strength in the face of an unfair world. Psychologist Fritz Redl (1966) also was fascinated by the positive qualities of troubled children. He once quipped that a book with a title such as The Virtues of Delinquent Children was needed, except that probably nobody would publish such a title. When professionals are drowned in negative information about children and families, they are unlikely to create viable plans for positive growth.

PROBLEMS OR POTENTIALS

A problem or issue can be perceived as a threat or as a challenge.

—Fred J. Hanna (2002, p. 96)

Today there is a resurgence of interest in treatment methods that recast problems as opportunities for learning and growth. Sparked by research on resilience and prevention, the American Psychological Association set a vision for the 21st century to create a "positive psychology" focusing on strengths instead of deficits (Seligman & Csikszentmihalyi, 2000). Likewise, therapists who focus more on solutions than on problems are able to enlist youth once seen as "resistant" and "dysfunctional" in the process of positive change (Berg, 1994).

In many ways children in conflict have learned to be stronger than youngsters from more tranquil backgrounds. Imagine the courage it must take for a child to stand in defiance of powerful adults. Treatment approaches that concentrate on the negative qualities of children obscure their resilience and resourcefulness. A rich array of tests can reliably document a child's limitations but are not particularly helpful in identifying what a child and family might be able to do well. Rather than viewing a child who does not show strength as deficient, one can assume this "deficiency" represents a lack of opportunities to master the skill (Rudolph & Epstein, 2000). When assessment and treatment are based on strengths, children and families are more likely to become full participants in the therapeutic process.

The recognition that children with problems also have strengths is an extension of the same discovery made earlier about families. Until recently, the prevailing view was that problem parents produced problem kids. Bruno Bettelheim's (1967) pronouncement that emotionally aloof "refrigerator mothers" caused autism was a low point in parent blaming. Even though these simplistic notions have been challenged by subsequent research, it is still fashionable to demonize parents of kids with problems.

Friesen and Stephens (1998) have documented how the strengths perspective is opening a broader range of opportunities for families. In the past, the traditional role has been *families as recipients of service,* as seen when expert professionals prescribe therapy or parent education. In contrast, the *families as allies* view assumes that parents with problems also have expertise that must be enlisted in problem solving. As family strengths become apparent, even more innovative roles are emerging. Families are stepping forward as advocates, policymakers, service providers, and researchers. But old ways die hard, and many still see families and children in conflict as passive recipients of treatment.

Today, many are glibly dropping the term *strength-based* to describe their approach with youth. However, few have reflected deeply on how different research and practice would be if we really believed in the potential of our most challenging young people. Erik Laursen (2000) defined strength-based interventions as including specific core beliefs and values such as these:

1. *Spotlight on strengths:* Each child and family has strengths. Our job is to help youth and families explore and develop these potentials and capabilities.

2. *Authentic relationships:* Children need strong positive bonds to adults that provide a sense of belonging and that set boundaries and positive expectations.

3. *Self-determination:* Children and families need to own problems and control their destiny so that they have a right to fully participate in planning and treatment.

4. *Positive change:* Labels and diagnoses often imply that current problems are permanent, but children and families can hope for and build a better future.

5. *Community resources:* Children and families are given supports that can include a web of wraparound services to meet specific growth needs.

6. *Cultural rootedness:* Respecting an individual's strengths includes respecting values and beliefs unique to race, gender, sexuality, and spiritual heritage.

7. *Service to others:* By showing concern for others, individuals rise above their own problems to contribute to the betterment of families, friends, and community.

A comprehensive example of strength-based intervention is the *wraparound model.* Instead of narrow programs offered for isolated problems, the needs of the youth or family determine the scope of the intervention. In the most intensive cases, resources from the broader community are mobilized to meet these needs. This mobilization requires an unconditional commitment to blend and create services for children, families, and schools (Eber, Nelson, & Miles, 1997). Focusing on the strengths of children and families allows creative interventions to be crafted. For example, a youth who has been labeled "manipulative" is recast as skillful in social interactions, and the goal is to use this strength to help the youth meet needs through more adaptive behavior. A growing body of research suggests that interventions involving families, peers, and schools produce more successful outcomes than approaches that target only one part of a child's ecology.[1]

Strength-based interventions focus on potentials while recognizing the need to address problems. Although it is important to know about any pathology, evidence is accumulating that indicates "strengths and capacities are the building blocks for change and should receive primary emphasis" (Duchnowski & Kutash, 1996, p. 102).

RESPECTFUL DISCIPLINE

Fritz Redl (1966) spent a long career pondering the type of discipline that would help children develop "controls from within." His clinical experience showed that, although punishment works with many children, it regularly backfires with many aggressive children. Punishment requires pain, but many youths are impervious to pain and only respond to punishments that reach the level of abuse. Punishment motivates not penitence but rather angry or avoidant responses against the punishing adult who replays past cruelty. Finally, youth who believe that punishment is unfair feel no remorse but become more skillful in avoiding detection.

Further research has clarified why punishment has unpredictable results (Sherman, 1993). If punishment is to be a deterrent, youth must have strong bonds to the person or community administering the sanctions. They then feel shame and are motivated to change their behavior. However, when violators view punishment as an unfair act by a hostile person, this triggers defiant indignation, which actually *increases* defiance. Motivated by the master emotion of angry pride, they resist change with a tenacity called the *unconquerable soul* in William Henley's 1875 poem *Invictus*. The good news is that youth caught up in conflict cycles motivated by angry defiance can be positively bonded to adults who give them the respect they so desperately pursue.

Discipline systems that do not consider the developmental maturity of a child will be off target much of the time. *Indulgent* adults seek to nurture children but fail to set high expectations or hold them accountable. By excusing problem behavior, they abdicate their role as adults and become "friends without influence." At the other extreme, *coercive* adults believe in holding youth accountable, but they fail to respect the young person's need for autonomy. The most effective management style avoids these two extremes. *Respectful* adults simultaneously nurture the needs of youth and maintain high expectations for positive behavior. They create strong helping alliances with youth that foster autonomy and responsibility (Gold & Osgood, 1992).

Developmental research indicates that parenting and guidance should be geared to the child's changing needs (Wood, 2000). As children mature, they need different types of adult support. Table 6.1 on page 118 summarizes how adult responsibilities should accommodate the child's changing needs.

The essential goal of working with families is to help parents build strengths so that they feel confident about their parenting skills and are able to cope with challenges in the family. Professionals should acknowledge parents' frustrations, explore their ideas about possible solutions, and help them focus on times they have been successful in managing their children's behavior (Webster-Stratton & Herbert, 1994).

Table 6.1

Matching Discipline to a Child's Maturity

Maturity Level	Growth Needs	Adult Responsibility
Infancy	Learning to trust	Provide total nurturance
Early childhood	Learning to cope	Teach skills and boundaries
Pre-adolescence	Developing autonomy	Guide activities and behavior
Adolescence	Caring for self and others	Be a mentor and advocate

The movement toward respectful discipline in schools is being implemented under the rubric "positive behavioral support." This support involves systems of intervention at three levels (Nelson, Scott, & Polsgrove, 1999):

Universal interventions are designed to create positive learning environments for all students. These interventions include positive discipline systems, pleasant learning environments, and relevant curricula and instruction. All staff should be able to set positive expectations and build respectful relationships with students.

Targeted interventions identify students who are at risk and make adjustments in the program. These interventions may include simple schedule changes, peer tutoring, or family involvement. More sophisticated interventions might include individual contracts, behavior plans, or social skills groups.

Intensive interventions are coordinated by a team of people serving a smaller population of students at risk, including those with emotional and behavioral needs. This may involve a wraparound plan involving school, family, and community resources such as mental health.

Developmental psychologists have long proposed that discipline problems be used for building conscience and self-control (Redl & Wineman, 1952; Hoffman, 2002). Problems at home and school provide opportunities to teach children how their behavior affects others. This teaching is the foundation of moral development. Following are 10 strategies for respectful discipline.

Strategy 1: Structuring for Success

Children do not perform well in coercive or chaotic settings. The adult's job is to manage the learning environment so that children are free to learn to manage themselves. Reasonable rules, predictable routines, and safe and orderly physical settings are prerequisites for optimal growth. Adults communicate high expectations for success in relationships infused with positive encouragement.

Strategy 2: Coaching for Competence

Problem behavior is an error in performance that offers a unique opportunity for an adult to coach the child in academic and social competence. True discipline involves mentoring a child in prosocial skills, values, and self-control. Children need adults who are on talent hunts, searching to find strengths where others see only weaknesses.

Strategy 3: Cultivating Caring Groups

When negative peer processes stir problem behavior, a change in group dynamics is in order. Group settings offer an opportunity to teach children to develop caring behavior and a sense of respect and fairness to all. Children who have trouble getting along in a group setting need training in prosocial skills rather than banishment or isolation.

Strategy 4: Boosting Attention and Affection

Children deprived of attention and affection are antagonistic, indifferent, or attention seeking. Communicating dislike triggers their fears of rejection. Thus adults need to be able to criticize behavior while providing unconditional regard for the youth. Girls and Boys Town research prescribes a ratio of four positive interactions to each critical interaction. The most powerful discipline occurs in a context of caring. However, if children gain attention only with negative behavior, deviance is reinforced.

Strategy 5: Boosting Morale and Motivation

Boredom often produces problem behavior. Youth engaged in exciting and relevant activities do not need to pursue fun and adventure through troublemaking. Youth are more highly motivated to finish the mundane when fun will follow. Still, they must learn to complete tasks that may not always be exciting.

Strategy 6: Respectful Reasoning

The most effective discipline is based on inductive reasoning, in which children learn to recognize how their behavior affects self and others. This reasoning enables them to feel empathy and appropriate guilt when they have hurt others and to repair relationships. But not all youth respond equally well to reasoning, and an adult who is constantly appealing to children or youth to change their behavior can become ineffective.

Strategy 7: Learner's Leeway

Certain behavior will run its course if the young person is allowed to self-correct. Some problems are best tolerated or ignored. If a youngster is seeking attention for misbehavior, even punishment can be a reward. Still, one should never ignore hurting behavior or actions that might lead to group defiance or contagion. No person has the right to hurt self or others.

Strategy 8: Hurdle Help

Children experiencing continual frustration and failure are primed for problem behavior. Restructuring tasks or breaking a large job into "just-manageable difficulties" avoids the extremes of anxiety or boredom. Success is a prerequisite for confidence. However, all learning involves error, and children need to develop the ability to fail courageously and try again.

Strategy 9: Humor Help

Good-natured humor reduces stress and fosters positive bonds among individuals and members of a group. It is a central coping strategy used by resilient people. Genuinely shared humor can completely reverse an emotional climate from negative to positive. Humor says, I enjoy being with you. But hostile or sarcastic humor has the opposite effect. Youth can be very sensitive to others' making fun of them or making light of their problems.

Strategy 10: Hope for the Hopeless

Behind various facades, many discouraged youth are spiritually adrift, struggling to find meaning and purpose in life. They need adults who believe in their absolute worth and potential in spite of behavioral difficulties. Adults who listen, enjoy youth, and provide them with opportunities to help and serve others give these young people proof of their value. Of course, some hopelessness reaches dangerous levels of depression that are unresponsive to routine encouragement. This depression and unresponsiveness should signal the need for specialized therapeutic intervention.

A number of promising programs have been produced to create safe and reclaiming schools in which there are no disposable kids (Brendtro, Ness, & Mitchell, 2001). The foundation of these programs is positive behavior support and respectful discipline. Building this foundation entails setting great expectations, using problems as teaching opportunities, and encouraging discouraged youth.

POSITIVE PEER CLIMATES

Wherever youth gather, a peer culture is born. Long before researchers studied negative peer influence, parents and teachers believed that one bad apple spoils the whole barrel. The main solutions to "bad apple blight" have been (1) protecting youth from negative peers and (2) transforming negative youth cultures. Both can be daunting tasks.

When antisocial individuals are brought together, they often build their friendships by trading tales of deviant exploits (Cairns & Cairns, 1994). For decades, research has shown that schools and treatment programs composed of adult-antagonistic youth turn into negative peer cultures or antisocial gangs (Polsky, 1962). For this reason, some propose totally separating "antisocial" youth from peers (Feldman, 1992; Henggeler et al., 1998; Dishion, McCord, & Poulin, 1999). Others believe that even difficult youth can be enlisted in creating positive group cultures (Polsky, 1962; Gold & Osgood, 1992; Goldstein & Glick, 1994). The latter view is a minority position; many assume it is impossible to form prosocial groups from the raw material of antisocial kids:

> In light of the mutually reinforcing effects of deviant peers on one another, school, juvenile justice, and community efforts that place troublesome youth together in special classrooms, treatment groups and community activities may exacerbate rather than ameliorate delinquent behavior. . . . It seems unreasonable to expect that a group of youth with behavioral problems will somehow generate prosocial values and group norms by interacting with one another. (Henggeler et al., 1998, pp. 129–130)

In the bad-apple theory, the goal is to forcibly extract youth from undesirable friends. This involves communicating the disadvantages of association with deviant peers and implementing "very unpleasant consequences when the youth contacts anti-social peers and positive consequences when the youth contacts positive peers" (Henggeler et al., 1998, p. 132). Given the power of peer relationships, it is necessary to "prepare the parents for battle." It is no easy task to keep youth from their friends, and those distrustful of adults are often highly loyal to their peers.

Many youths are served in separate schools and residential settings where their main contacts are with other high-risk youths. Underground cultures can be very strong in such settings because peers provide a rate of reinforcement of 9 to 1 compared with adult staff (Buehler, Patterson, & Furniss, 1966). These negative cultures can sabotage the most elaborate treatment intervention. As incidents of school violence have shown, even public schools in privileged communities can spawn destructive peer cultures.

Contrary to the bad-apple paradigm, with skilled adult guidance, youths are in fact able to "generate prosocial values and group norms." This strategy requires approaching youth as resources instead of adversaries to be outmaneuvered. Successful programs to transform negative peer climates have been developed in both school and treatment settings.

In hundreds of schools nationwide, the Resolving Conflict Creatively Program (RCCP) mobilizes students, staff, and families to develop peacemaking values and honor diversity. RCCP has reversed negative peer cultures in many once-violent schools. The first RCCP model was implemented in a school in which the principal had been killed by a stray bullet from a youth's gun. The goal of RCCP is to create a climate of respect that permeates the school. Students and staff manage conflicts with a problem-solving approach (Lantieri & Patti, 1996). These strategies reverse negative peer norms that validate violence.

Because school violence has been traced to bullying and peer harassment, there is a strong interest in transforming these negative school climates. Codes of silence permit peer intimidation to reign. Comprehensive interventions involve all staff and parents as well as bullies, victims, and bystanders. The most profound change to the group climate comes when the "silent majority" is aroused and embraces the norm that bullying is not acceptable in their school (Olweus, 1996). In working with bullies, the goal is to redirect their power into positive avenues. Often such youth are highly skilled at intimidating, conning, or controlling others. They may have an abundance of self-confidence and ill-gotten self-esteem coming from wielding power over others. In many cases, bullies can be transformed into prosocial leaders. Bullies who are more disturbed may need additional interventions targeting their thinking errors (Gibbs, Potter, Goldstein, & Brendtro, 1996). Finally, scapegoats need strategies for dealing with teasing and harassment. When adults and students join forces to keep schools safe, major reductions in antisocial behavior follow (Olweus, 1996).

The Positive Peer Culture (PPC) program (Vorrath & Brendtro, 1985) enlists youth in helping one another. It uses problem-solving groups in which youth with an adult leader provide support and respectfully challenge hurting behavior. PPC has been shown to be effective in creating safe environments in treatment programs, even for incarcerated youth (Gold & Osgood, 1992). An extension of the PPC model is the EQUIP program (Gibbs, Potter, & Goldstein, 1995), which adds formal training in thinking errors, moral development, and social skills training; this "equips" youth to be more effective peer helpers. Research on EQUIP also shows sustained positive changes with youth in peer-helping groups (Gibbs, Potter, Goldstein, & Brendtro, 1998).

A growing body of research shows that well-designed peer treatment programs can have predictable positive effects on participants (Giacobbe, Traynelis-Yurek, & Laursen, 1999). Youth significantly improve on measures of achievement, self-esteem, and prosocial values and behavior. Most encouraging is recent evidence that peer-helping models can create safe, positive environments, even with antisocial youth. Martin Gold (1974) was an early critic of peer group treatment. He changed his view as a result of his extensive research on peer-helping groups in treatment settings for troubled and troubling adolescents (Gold & Osgood, 1992):

> The essential question was whether or not programs of this sort were indeed able to establish positive youth cultures. The research evidence is very encouraging. Youth were uniformly found to view their living environments as safe. Moreover, stronger youth groups, with greater perceived autonomy in their settings, were generally regarded by youth and staff as more positive and prosocial. . . . This set of findings was an important validation because it meant that the conditions, at least, for effective group treatment were present. (p. 212)

A group of irresponsible youth cannot bootstrap a positive culture alone. They need guidance from committed adults trained in methods for building caring peer cultures. At the core of communities of respect is the powerful, overriding core value that no person—youth or adult—will be permitted to hurt another and that individuals who don't help are hurting. There are intensive group-oriented interventions specifically designed to transform negative cultures into positive climates (NDK, 2003; Vorrath & Brendtro, 1985; Gibbs, Potter, Goldstein, & Brendtro, 1996). Here we highlight four methods that have been applied in a variety of educational and treatment settings. The goal is to build individual and group value systems of caring and mutual respect. Youth do not change easily, so these methods require activism by the adult. Several cautions in using these strategies are also noted.

Strategy 1: Reversing Responsibility

The initial goal is to get youth to take responsibility for their behavior. This is a formidable barrier; blaming others is an art form with many children. Because youth are expert at shifting responsibility, adults must be more skillful and tenacious at reversing responsibility. This is done with simple verbal interactions:

Student: Why should I care? Nobody cares about me.

Staff: Then perhaps it's up to you to take charge of your own life.

Student: John is such a jerk. He always insults everybody's mother.

Staff: I am sure the group will want to help John with his problems, but you don't have to let him suck you into his garbage.

Student: *(Shifts responsibility)* What do you expect? My parents are both drunks.

Staff: *(Reverses responsibility)* Is Tony trying to tell the group that everybody with alcoholic parents decides to abuse alcohol?

As adults model reversing responsibility, young people begin to use this approach with irresponsible peers. Reversal is a special case of respectful confrontation. As one youth said of this technique, "It's like they hold up a mirror; and whatever the problem is, you find the answer to it somewhere inside of yourself!"

A caution: The goal is not to become embroiled in testy arguments but to communicate in a simple, respectful way the belief that the youth is mature enough to assume responsibility. However, high expectations for positive behavior should never interfere with expressing empathy for a youth who is hurting. Still, do not permit youths to be victims or dodge responsibility.

Strategy 2: Confronting with Concern

The word *confront* has two possible meanings. It can mean to attack, as to confront another in battle, or to face a challenge. The latter definition applies here. Youth who enjoy hurtful behavior are unlikely to change unless the reality of what they are doing becomes very clear. Most do not suffer from excess guilt but from a lack of guilt. Only when youth understand how they have hurt themselves and others with their actions will they be motivated to change.

There is no more powerful method of discipline than to face those who care deeply about you. Still, criticism must be balanced with positive approval. The concept of a "sandwich" style of criticism comes from Girls and Boys Town. A critical comment is wrapped in two supportive ones, as seen in this example:

Support: Maria has been helping other group members with their problems.

Criticism: However, she still hasn't faced her own problem of misleading others.

Support: Maria soon will show the courage to accept the group's help.

Goldstein (1993) finds role playing to be a useful means of giving youth the strength to receive criticism, express complaints, and deal with someone who is angry without either shrinking or counterattacking. Youth learn to listen openly and actively, to express understanding of the other person's feeling and thinking, and to acknowledge areas of agreement and honest disagreement.

A caution: Confrontation rooted in animosity is a type of violence. Hostile, demeaning confrontation quickly destroys the trust essential for a positive culture. (See Allan's account in Chapter 9 of mistreatment by peers in a "treatment" setting.)

Strategy 3: Making Caring Fashionable

The central ethos in a truly positive peer climate is that helping is valued and anything that hurts another is devalued. This is quite a change for many youth groups in which caring is not fashionable. Except for loyalty to a gang member or a very narrow circle of friends, giving or getting help may be seen as being weak. The technique of "relabeling" challenges this self-centered thinking.

For example, youth may describe wild behavior in terms suggesting that it is strong, cool, smart, or sophisticated. Instead of attacking a group member's show of strength ("You aren't as strong as you think"), the message links strength to helping: "A person as strong as you will really be able to become a great group member. Helping takes strength."

Relabeling can be used to elevate positive behavior and to de-romanticize hurting behavior. For example, if truancy has an exciting quality for a youth, it could be relabeled "imma-ture," perhaps "playing games of hide-and-seek." Likewise, if stealing is seen as "slick," it might be relabeled "sneaky and dumb."

A caution: Any use of negative labels should refer only to the person's behavior, never to the person. The message must come through as "This is a very immature way of acting for someone as mature as you." By pairing positive statements that recognize the dignity of a person with critical statements about behavior, we communicate powerfully without eliciting unnecessary resistance.

Strategy 4: Cultivating Esprit de Corps

In some group settings, a preoccupation with "treatment" and behavior control preempts positive activities. Youth need rich group experiences to enable maturation and growth. Holding positive experiences hostage to behavior is like starving patients so they will want to get well. Two major types of group activity have been very effective in building a positive group culture. *Adventure learning experiences* bond youth together in meeting a common challenge. *Service learning activities* invite young people to reach out to help in the community.

Examples of activities that combine both adventure and service are seen each year at the Reclaiming Youth Seminars.[2] Groups of youth from treatment programs and alternative schools from the United States, Canada, and Australia have traveled to these professional conferences with their staffs. They are always excited to journey to these destinations, where fresh experiences await. The consumptive element in such a trip is balanced by service activities. One group of Michigan teens does volunteer recreation with young children from the Pine Ridge reservation. Such activities create a strong esprit de corps and get youth hooked on helping.

A final concern: In peer group programs, the lines between best practice and malpractice must be very clear (Brendtro & Ness, 1982). Youth should have no power to punish, harass, or intimidate peers but only a license to help. A brief Internet search finds disturbing references to "positive peer culture" in such unlikely places as the home pages for boot camps. Most programs referred to as boot camps are based on peer coercion rather than concern. Effective peer culture programs follow the key assumptions of strength-based treatment. Staff model caring and respect in all interactions. High expectations require demanding responsibility instead of obedience. Youth become co-workers with adults in creating a caring environment.

"MY INDEPENDENCE DAY"
Kevin's Story

Some youth have a negative resilience in which they display their considerable talent and tenacity by defying adults. Kevin was a 15-year-old who was considered beyond the control of his family and teachers.[3] He was declared incorrigible by the court and placed in a series of residential programs, but he was kicked out of six placements in eight months because he was "unresponsive to treatment." Kevin used all of his strengths to battle anyone who tried to exert authority over him.

———

Things were deteriorating at home, and I had a night of fighting with my parents. I don't even know what started it. Everybody wanted to be right, nobody backed down, and we said meaner and meaner things to one another. I said, "I hate you, bitch, go to hell." She said, "You're the one who's going to end up in hell some day." She would cry, but since she was hurting me, we were even. My mom said we were going for counseling. I didn't see my suitcase packed in the back of the station wagon.

At the outpatient center, we visited with a counselor who gave a few tests, after which my parents said I would be staying. Then I said, "I hate your guts. I'm never coming home again." I was only there for a couple of weeks. They gave me lots of tests, even a brain scan, to see if I was crazy. I wasn't, of course. Shortly before my release, I was placed in isolation for assaulting staff. They strapped me down, and I laughed at them and tried to show them they couldn't do anything to me. When they left the room, I got out of the restraints. "I'm Houdini!" I shouted, and I banged on the windows. They recommended I be sent to a boys' ranch, but I refused.

Back at home, the trouble continued. I thought I would avoid conflict with my parents and have a better time if I could live at a friend's house. I'd say, "Send me away. I don't want to live here!" They gave me what I wanted. However, I found I wasn't going to be able to live with my friends. They brought evidence against me to send me away.

I was sent away to a group home called Welcome House. I was mad at my parents for what they did, and felt lonely and depressed. Staff welcomed me with "Your stay here can be a living hell, or it can be good for you. It is up to you." That really made me mad. This was a peer group program.

Other residents would act like they cared about me, but really it was an act so they could get out. I tried to walk away from the group, but they would throw me on the ground and restrain me. I would think, "Fight 'em. Don't let them push you around." One staff member said, "Maybe you like being restrained, Kevin. What's the matter; were you physically or sexually abused as a child? Or maybe you perpetrated against somebody else!" I was furious because it wasn't true, and I fought them that much more.

I thought the staff were all idiots, but I talked to some kids I trusted. The best thing about this time was that I learned how to help others. I learned I had more power than I thought; my words meant something. I could be a leader, and I used it to get them to be negative or positive, depending on how I felt that day. Once, my group leader said I was the best helper in the group.

I watched other people carefully to see what got them in trouble and what got them angry. If I felt some staff were unfair to me, I would find out something about their life, and I would use it by cutting them. They would get angry and show more of their weak spots. When I realized I was not going to be getting out soon, I started trying to provoke the staff and create anarchy among the kids. The last night, I grabbed a fire extinguisher and sprayed it around to juice up the group. They restrained me, and I attacked peers. The group leader was called in. He said I was going to be sent away to a forestry camp for a year and a half. "You will never see your family again, because you ruined everything." I got really angry and said, "That's not true; they love me!" I wasn't sure of it though. That time I was sent to River City.

This institution had federal cases from all over the country—kids who had committed serious crimes. I sat in cells for three weeks and all I could think about was that maybe I would never see my parents again. I was going crazy in there, with a mattress in a corner without sheets and cracks in the floor with bugs in them. I wanted to be dead so I didn't have to go through what was happening. The court said I was going to remain at River City and be placed in their group treatment program. I had problems with my group. I felt they didn't care and would just cut me down. When I refused to talk about the problems in group, staff brought in a video camera and started recording my behavior. I told them they couldn't do this legally without my permission, but they said, "So we're breaking the law; we're just protecting ourselves. You lost your rights when you came in here." I was put back into the time-out room, and I put on a show for the camera, slamming my fist into the wall. I fought them any way I could.

They sent me to detention pending another placement. For two months I was not in school. I kept getting into a lot of trouble and was confined to my room a lot. They decided to send me to Heartland Health Services. When I discovered some kids had already put in three years at Heartland, I was afraid I might be stuck in that place for a long time. "Whoa," I thought. "This looks like a mental hospital." I decided this place was not for me. One day when I was defying staff, they stuck me in an isolation room and came in to restrain me. I gave a staff member a bloody nose and said that the next one would be harder. He ran. After doing this stuff for a couple of weeks, they put me on medication to change my behavior. Mind over matter; I was pissed and decided these drugs were not going to change me!

Psychologists would take me for tests and interviews. I thought they were trying to prove I was crazy, and they would ask me to check off lists of problems. I didn't like them and wouldn't share my problems. I became an expert at building walls to keep away people who wanted to help me. My most successful wall builder was to say things to piss them off so they wouldn't want to be around me. They tried reverse psychology on me. If I had trouble with the group, instead of punishing me, they would say, "Oh, it's too stressful. We will give you your own staff." They took me to the nicest day room in the facility with a TV, couch, everything. They thought they could trick me into wanting to go back to the group. I just played video games all day and watched TV. It was a blast. I remember that they had point sheets for prizes and treats. I thought it was B.S., but they

could trick the little kids with it. I said I didn't care if I got
points.

By surprise the cops came, pulled a chain around my
waist and under my crotch, and cuffed me to the chain. They
locked shackles on my feet and transported me 300 miles in
a police car. For the next month I was in maximum security.
A guy from Sunset Boys' Ranch came to visit me. I told him
if he took me, I would make his f——ing place a living hell.
He said, "We'll get back to you, Kevin," and I never saw him
again.

> All attempts to change Kevin had been variations of try-
> ing to break a wild pony. The director of the detention
> center decided on another tactic. He created a team of
> people who tried to forge a respectful alliance with
> Kevin. Staff made every effort not to get into power
> struggles or to reciprocate hostility. The first opportunity
> for connecting with Kevin came when he voiced his
> concern about the court's plans to send him out of
> state. He knew that some youth in the detention center
> were enrolled in a 90-day treatment program. Kevin
> joined with staff in writing a letter to his judge propos-
> ing he stay here in a three-month treatment program
> for his "authority problems." The judge approved the
> plan. After several rocky weeks, Kevin began to show
> positive growth. He engaged with teachers in school
> and began to develop new connections with his family.
> As he approached release, Kevin reflected on the posi-
> tive changes he was experiencing.

Before coming here, everybody else had always come on
with a "You better get your act together or else." In the other
places I was fighting against the counselors and staff. Here I
was working with them. I was treated like an equal, not one
who was inferior. Because these staff did not try to over-
power me, we seldom got into real power struggles. When I
wanted to be right, even if I was stating some outrageous
opinion, bullshitting them, they would listen instead of challenging or interrupting me. Once, after a very difficult session following my first visit home, I said, "It was at times like

this that I got kicked out of those other places." I had found that I could talk my way through even very stressful situations.

My counselors were always bringing in some saying that had a lesson in it for me. Robert Louis Stevenson once said, "It isn't the cards that you are dealt but how you play the hand you hold." I knew that just because I didn't get myself a dad when I was born, and I had trouble with both of my stepfathers, still that is them and I am me. I could mope around about that all my life, but crying about not having a dad will not get me one. I have to learn to forgive and forget. One day I was given a card with a quote from Carl Jung: "Where love rules, there is no will to power, and where power predominates, there love is lacking."

I always wanted to be in charge of everybody in my life, and my trying to be in charge was hurting other people. When you quit needing to always fight for power with others, you are free to love.

I could see that I was changing. I wanted to change, but I was scared to change. I didn't know how it would be if I wasn't like I used to be. I wish I had more teachers and counselors who really believed in me. Perhaps it would have not taken this much time and pain to come to where I am today. But I think that now I can survive even if some of my teachers are not as interested or understanding as I would like. I will have to work to avoid slipping into my tendency to blame them and succeed in spite of them. I need to work for myself, not to please them.

Next year I will be a senior in high school, and I am trying to get a more positive attitude about school. Right now I am scared because I do not know how students at my own school will treat me when I come back. Will they accept me as a friend? When they ask me where I have been for a year, what do I say? Will they tease me and make fun of me? Will their parents tell them not to hang around with me? Will they make up stories and rumors about me? I know any of these things might happen. With patience and persistence, I expect to be able to work this out. In the end, it is not what other people might think or say about me that is the most important, but what I think about myself.

Tomorrow is December 20, and I will be moving back home with my family. For me, July 4 is no longer Independence Day. From now on, December 20 will be my Independence Day.

NOTES

[1] Promising approaches are described in a volume edited by Epstein, Kutash, and Duchnowski (1998). Prominent among methods with research support is multisystemic treatment, developed by Scott Henggeler and colleagues (1998).

[2] For further information on Reclaiming Youth Seminars, visit **www.reclaiming.com**.

[3] Adapted from an article written by this youth under a pseudonym (Kevin, 1994), printed with permission of *Reclaiming Children and Youth*. A companion article describes the treatment strategies staff used to help Kevin turn around his life (Brendtro & Banbury, 1994).

CHAPTER SEVEN
Crisis as Opportunity

Most adults want to help kids in conflict but just do not know how. Award-winning novelist Tobias Wolff wrote *This Boy's Life,* which recounts his own childhood abuse and rebellion. Wolff cites an occasion when his frustrated mother asked the parish priest, Father Carl, to talk with him. Father Carl invited young Toby for a walk by the river. Toby played along by politely feigning cooperation:

> [Father Carl] asked me if I wanted to make my mother unhappy.
>
> I said, "No."
>
> "But you're making her unhappy, aren't you?"
>
> "I guess."
>
> "No guessing to it. You are."
>
> He looked over at me. "So why don't you stop, why don't you stop?"
>
> I didn't answer right away for fear of seeming merely agreeable. I wanted to appear to give his question some serious thought.
>
> "All right," I said. "I'll try."
>
> I was not available to be reached. I was in hiding. I had left a dummy in my place to look sorry and make promises but I was nowhere in the neighborhood and Father Carl knew it.[1]

Even adults with formal professional training have trouble connecting with "difficult clients" (Hanna, 2002). In spite of a sincere desire to reach young people, they don't know how to get around the defenses that have been so carefully constructed, often over a period of many years. All professionals need effective strategies to disengage from adversarial roles and connect with youth in crisis.

OUT OF THE ASHES

Schools, courts, and mental health programs are often overwhelmed by youth in conflict. In an official policy statement, the American Academy of Child and Adolescent Psychiatry (2002) declares, "Within the review of crisis behavior lie opportunities to prevent their recurrence . . . to create a 'Phoenix out of the ashes'" (p. 19S).

In the traditional deficit view, a crisis is a calamity. From a strengths perspective, a crisis offers a unique opportunity for reinforcing relationships and coping skills. But this requires strategies for interrupting conflict and using crises as learning situations.

Disengaging from Hostility

If crises are to become teaching opportunities, adults must disentangle themselves from angry, adversarial conflicts with youth. Rather than be drawn into Tit for Tat reactions, adults must treat problem behavior as errors in responding rather than purposeful defiance (Ducharme, Atkinson, & Poulton, 2000).

Defusing conflict begins with a personal choice not to fight with a youth. This does not mean becoming weak or permissive. Instead, as Nick Long (2000) observes, one decides to act like a thermostat rather than a thermometer. A thermometer goes up or down depending on the surrounding climate. If we allow ourselves to become overheated—or turned off—by a youth's behavior, we become like thermometers under control of the youth. But a thermostat is a more sophisticated instrument. It registers temperature like a thermometer, but then makes the necessary adjustment to keep the climate in balance. When a student's emotions kindle, we can calm them down. When a youth is down, we can help bring him or her back up.

Skillfully handling conflict is a "double struggle" of managing one's own private logic and emotions while trying to calm a youth. Clinical and research studies suggest practical strategies that are foundation skills in defusing angry conflict.[2]

Strategy 1: Never Take Anger Personally

Conflict cycles operate like mirror images, in which both parties believe they have been provoked and both feel justified in the righteous rage. When we take anger personally, we assume the mind-set of victims, and we step on a slippery slope. To avoid the mentality of "violated" victim requires controlling the private logic by which we interpret conflict. One should think of an alternative explanation for a person's anger other than that the person is intentionally being offensive. The sooner in a conflict cycle that empathy is used to crowd out blaming thoughts, the easier it is to de-escalate the cycle.

Strategy 2: Monitor Your Own Emotional Arousal

Be aware of internal cues that anger or fear is reaching a disruptive level. If you notice rancor in your voice, this signals that emotions are in charge and it is time to cool down or back away from the interaction. Sometimes empathy statements can break the cycle of hostility. However, adults may not want to appear weak or be manipulated by angry youth, and so they often persist in fruitless disagreements. This won't calm either party in this dance of disturbance. Backing away from conflict does not mean that the incident is closed. Rather, the communication is being postponed until calmer minds prevail. Disengagement is not a sign of weakness but one of strength and self-control.

Strategy 3: Monitor and Defuse a Youth's Agitation

In a brewing conflict, an alert adult carefully tracks a youth's emotional arousal to avoid explosive outcomes. Rodney had overheard a phone conversation between his foster mother and a social worker, and he suspected he was about to be kicked out of his foster home. He arrived at school agitated and paranoid and soon was sent to the office. It became clear that Rodney believed school staff were a party in plotting against him for his abandonment. Rodney said he was so furious that he might break the windows out of the conference room and jump. Instead of confrontation, he needed a strongly supportive statement: "We can understand why you are so mad. You have every right to know what is going to happen to you." Rodney was ready for battle but not for empathy, and his hostility melted into sobs. One can imagine an alternative scenario if adults had moved to physically contain Rodney and escalated this crisis into a full-scale restraint.

Strategy 4: Allow Sufficient Time for Cooling Down

In a natural course, intense emotion spikes and then decays. Time is our ally. Attempts to argue or reason with an agitated person will prolong and escalate anger. If the helper notices tension in his or her own voice or nonverbal behavior, or if the presence of the adult is stirring rage in the youth, it may be better to temporarily acquiesce or withdraw. If the helper can communicate true warmth instead of hostility, then "joining" with the person who is angry usually will defuse tension. In general, the best strategy is to offer support with a tone of strength and compassion to communicate that violence is neither a necessary nor an acceptable way of resolving conflict.

Strategy 5: Debrief Following Crisis Incidents

Just because the storm appears to have passed does not mean that hostility is defused. Angry people who stew in the private logic of feeling violated or disrespected can work themselves up with plans to get even and retaliate (Sapolsky, Stocking, & Zillman, 1977). By helping an angry youth rethink a crisis event, guilt or rancor can be lessened and the youth is given an opportunity to learn effective coping. Standards on physical confinement and restraint now require debriefing after critical events (JCAHCO, 2001; AACAP, 2002). Life Space Crisis Intervention (LSCI) is specifically designed for this purpose and will be discussed in detail in the following section.

Strategy 6: Model a Forgiving Spirit

There is no greater act of generosity than giving by forgiving. People who make amends communicate benevolence instead of malevolence. But some adults are slow to forgive a youth who has crossed them, and even less likely to apologize for any part they may have had in a conflict. If an adult realizes that a conflict situation could have been handled in a more tactful manner, a prompt, genuine apology often de-escalates anger. Adults who are too proud to apologize are often obsessed with proving their toughness. In a battle of wills, both parties see backing down as a sign of weakness. The adult has a unique opportunity to demonstrate that truly strong people can walk away from a fight with dignity, a skill all youth need to learn.

Talking about anger is not the only way of defusing it. Some youth respond well to diversionary activities, humor, and re-immersion in positive relationships. Because anger is a highly unpleasant emotion, there is a natural motivation to restore harmony. For both youth and adult, ruminating about hostility is highly counterproductive. The age-old advice is forever current: Never let the sun set on your anger.

Learning from Crisis Events

A crisis is an event that causes emotional conflict and threatens a person's ability to cope effectively. In a severe crisis, the person has feelings of distress, confusion, and loss of control. Handled poorly, crisis situations can metastasize into trauma. Traditional crisis intervention programs focus on physical safety and de-escalation and should be basic training for all who work with potentially volatile children.[3] But beyond defusing a crisis, the challenge is to break self-defeating patterns of behavior. This requires advanced training.

Nicholas Long and colleagues have developed a comprehensive curriculum for training adults to communicate with youth in conflict and use crisis as a teaching and treatment tool (Long, Wood, & Fecser, 2001). Life Space Crisis Intervention uses naturally occurring problems to teach youth more effective coping skills. Crises become opportunities to help youth learn alternatives to aggressive, disrespectful, or self-destructive behavior. LSCI is useful to educators, counselors, and other professionals who deal with youth in mental health, juvenile justice, and faith-based and community agencies. These people need practical, proven strategies that work in the real world, on the front lines of the child's "life space." This is not therapy on a couch but therapy on the run.[4]

Fritz Redl found descriptive terms such as *oppositional* and *conduct problem* to be of little value in developing behavioral interventions. Instead, he built an entire system of therapy around diagnosing significant events in the child's life. A life event is best understood by knowing how it was experienced and interpreted, rather than viewing behavior through the distorted "optics" of a particular discipline (Csikszentmihalyi, 1990, p. 26). Sticking to events avoids the trap of confusing clinical jargon. People without psychological training can describe events in detail. Children, including those with cognitive disabilities, can communicate most effectively by relating stories (Baker & Gersten, 2000).

Redl, like his mentor, August Aichhorn (1935), would engage youth in detailed discussion of an event to decode the meaning of the behavior:

> How does it start? Where does it end? Try to translate into an actual anecdotal incident—an "event system." There is no other way to get at the clinical facts. . . . Stick to the here and now, the actual process, the demarcated event and then you will begin to understand. (Redl, 1994, p. 53)

A person who shares emotionally charged life events opens a window to his or her world. Exchanging stories also is a prime means of social bonding. Unfortunately, many interviewers either interrupt respondents when they break into stories or disregard the importance of this narrative (Bruner, 1990). By exploring events of importance to a child, we get a sample of how that youngster thinks, perceives, and feels. People do not reinvent themselves with each new challenge. Thus timelines of events reveal a youth's typical coping style, whether constructive or self-defeating.

LIFE SPACE THERAPY

Every crisis presents the opportunity for psychological growth and the danger of psychological deterioration.

—Gerald Caplan (1964, p. 53)

Helping adults need a "road map" for the frequently perplexing mission of communicating with kids in crisis. In this section, we describe the rationale and research behind Life Space Crisis Intervention, also called Life Space Therapy. A full continuum of strategies is available, ranging from crisis de-escalation to therapy for long-term change. The depth of the interventions is determined by needs of the youth as well as the setting and staff training.[5] For example, some school staff use LSCI as a means of supporting a youth in time of crisis. In more intensive treatment settings, LSCI becomes a model of strength-based therapy.

Life Space Therapy progresses in a sequence of six therapeutic strategies that build on one another. A given intervention entails some or all of these strategies, and greater dosages of intervention provide increasingly intensive treatment.[6] These strategies are described next with examples of supportive research.

Strategy 1: De-Escalate the Crisis Event

With extreme fear or anger, the brain's centers for rational thinking and positive emotions shut down (LeDoux & Phelps, 2000). A youth whose synapses are in survival mode is not ready to solve problems. Thus in times of emotional duress, the first priority is to calm the turbulence. If the adult reciprocates angry emotional displays, negativity only escalates in both parties.

Providing support and empathy disentangles one from the enemy role and de-escalates emotions. Leaving the person to cool off in isolation can fuel anger and alienation, but being with a youth in time of crisis begins a supportive alliance. Helping a youth regain self-control and a sense of dignity is itself a significant therapeutic goal. The next step is to understand what caused the problem.

Strategy 2: Clarify the Timeline of What Happened

The adult avoids being judgmental and seeks to enlist the young person in a problem-solving process. The youth is invited to share his or her account of what happened to produce the crisis. The adult helps the student clarify what happened through a respectful process of Socratic questioning. This provides important data about the child's reality, whether accurate or distorted. As a timeline of the problem unfolds and is clarified, the adult learns how this youth thinks, feels, and behaves.

Some question whether talking to a youth in crisis might reinforce negative behavior by drawing attention to it. In fact, many angry youth initially find discussing their problems with adults to be aversive, not rewarding. If adults in the past have been coercive or disrespectful, this new adult will be cast in the role of hated authority. However, whether a youth is seeking attention or trying to avoid communication, the goal is to use the crisis as an occasion for positive learning.

Humans seem to be genetically programmed to confide in others in times of crisis (Pennebaker, 1990). Presumably, reaching out to others has survival value by securing support, empathy, and advice. The greater the distress, the greater the need to talk about it. People who "tell their story" reduce their stress and bond with others. Although we cannot change past events, we can seek to understand and learn from them. Humans attribute personal meanings to experience, and we become the stories we tell (Meichenbaum & Fong, 1993).

If a problem turns out to be a simple misunderstanding or rule infraction that can be routinely managed, staff may choose to end the intervention, having provided "emotional first aid." However, if this appears to be a self-defeating pattern, the next step is to determine the purpose of the maladaptive behavior.

Strategy 3: Diagnose the Meaning of Behavior

There are many systems for assessing childhood behavior. Prominent is the DSM psychiatric model, which classifies behavior patterns as *mental disorders*, such as anxiety disorder or conduct disorder (American Psychiatric Association, 2000). Alternative psychological models use statistical studies to identify *behavior dimensions,* such as withdrawal or aggression (Achenbach, 2000). Both approaches are more descriptive than prescriptive and may cast little light on the meaning of the behavior, the strengths of the child, or the specific interventions needed (Scotti, Morris, McNeil, & Hawkins, 1996).

In LSCI, behaviors such as aggression or withdrawal are seen as *coping strategies* that serve some function for the person. Behavior observation and dialogue with the youth identify the goal of the behavior. The diagnostic categories are tied to specific prescriptive interventions:

Imported problems. Behavior out of proportion to the situation may be carried over from prior conflicts. Thus problems encountered at home or in peer relationships may be imported to school. Zillman (1993) documented the residual carryover effects of earlier stress or trauma that primes angry responses to later, minor irritations.

Errors in perception. Heightened emotions or biased thinking cause distortions of reality. Dodge and Somberg (1987) found that the hostile biases of certain children are exaggerated by situations in which they perceive some threat to the self. Such distortions of perception can evoke and maintain aggressive or defensive behavior.

Limited social skills. Some youngsters have the right goal, such as wanting to make friends, but go about it in the wrong way. These youth need social skills instruction. Goldstein (1999) cataloged a range of methods for teaching prosocial competencies.

Exploited by others. Youth may be misled or bullied by peers who set them up or exploit them. Olweus (1993) pioneered research on school bullies and their victims, whom he calls "whipping boys." Vulnerable students need support and skills to extricate themselves from victim roles.

Delinquent pride. Some youth derive satisfaction from exploiting others. They feel little guilt about hurting others and are comfortable with antisocial behavior. Gibbs, Potter, and Goldstein (1995) outline interventions to confront these patterns of antisocial thinking, values, and behavior.

Impulsiveness and guilt. Some young people act without thinking and then feel terrible. Such youth may have a conscience and values but lack self-control. When they have problems, guilt and shame make them feel inadequate and worthless. These youth need encouragement to strengthen their self-efficacy and develop self-worth (Bandura, 1995).

With a working hypothesis about the meaning of behavior, one is prepared to proceed with more intensive therapeutic strategies.[7] There are three additional therapeutic reclaiming strategies when more intense intervention is sought.

Strategy 4: Promote Insight and Accountability

Once the adult diagnoses a pattern, the logical next step is to help the youth gain understanding and ownership of the problem. Otherwise, "no win" patterns of behavior are likely to continue. Insight is not depth psychology but a concrete recognition of how behavior hurts others and leads to self-defeating outcomes. Carl Rogers (1939) observed that insight involves self-objectivity and responsibility for one's behavior. Because children lack such insight, life's adversities are amplified as children deny or exaggerate faults.

Because past events cannot be changed, one way of coping with trauma is to learn to understand and reinterpret the event in a more meaningful way (Salovey, Bedell, Detweiler, & Mayer, 2000). Youth whose lives have been violated need to learn that dangers that once threatened them no longer exist, and that there are better ways of coping and achieving their goals (Edelstien, 1990). A person who recognizes the self-defeating nature of a pattern of behavior is motivated to change.

Strategy 5: Teach Prosocial Coping Skills

Good intentions are not sufficient; youth need specific behavioral skills to overcome problems. A boy victimized by peers may need assertiveness training. A girl who enjoys intimidating others may benefit from empathy training. An impulsive youth needs skills for developing self-control. Many skills can be taught spontaneously in the natural situation. Alternatively, an impressive array of social skills curricula is available.[8] For example, Warger and Rutherford (1996) have worked with special and general education teachers from around the country to implement a classroom-based approach to teaching social skills with emphasis on responsibility and respect.

A particular challenge is motivating resistant youth to participate in skills training. When interventions seem relevant to youth, they will be more motivated to participate than when adults assign arbitrary, contrived tasks. One promising approach is to have youth learn skills so they in turn can teach these to peers or younger children (Gibbs, Potter, & Goldstein, 1995). All young people have a natural desire to find the most effective strategies for coping with the challenges in their lives. Artificial training in hothouse environments will not survive the chill of life in the real world.

Strategy 6: Transfer Learning to the Life Space

Lessons learned in any teaching or counseling intervention need to transfer to the relationships in family, school, peer group, and community. Most immediately, the task is to help a youth who was in crisis reenter the life space where the problem began. But beyond this short-term adaptation, we seek enduring, long-term gains. The greatest frustration with any treatment method has been the lack of carryover of learning after external controls and supports are withdrawn. Goldstein and Martens (2000) suggest that earlier notions of "train and hope" are not viable, and we must teach for transfer. Efforts to build self-control are more likely to generalize than attempts to instill obedience. Repeated dosages of intervention are more effective than isolated treatments. The most powerful results come when the focus is not just on changing the youth but on creating changes across the youth's immediate life space (Greenberg, Bierman, Cole, Dodge, Lochman, & McMahon, 1998; Schoenwald, Borduin, & Henggeler, 1998). When teaching or treatment gives the youth practical coping solutions for naturally occurring problems, transfer is more likely. Finally, when placement changes or helping terminates, the young person needs trusted adults and positive peers who will support the gains made.

Ceremonies offer powerful means to celebrate passages and achievements. These mark the changes and growth that have occurred in a young person's life. Other youth can also vicariously participate in this success and see a model of positive change. Lighthouse School on Beaver Island in Lake Michigan serves at-risk students. Each semester all students come to the mainland for a graduation ceremony. As veterans share their successes, new students envision what they might one day accomplish. A veteran named Travis told of one such success:

> Travis went to the podium and said, "When I came to Lighthouse, I had never had a brother before, and here I found one. I want my new brother to stand up." A 250-pound boy, Kip, shyly rose to his feet. "Kip, come stand up here in front of everybody. Now hold your fist in the air." Kip complied with some shyness. "They say that the human heart is the size of a fist," said Travis. He then asked half a dozen other boys to surround Kip, and each held his fist up to Kip's. "Now, do you see that heart in the middle that draws all the other hearts to it? Put all of those hearts together and that's the size of Kip's heart."

This discussion has highlighted the reclaiming strategies in Life Space Therapy. A summary of an actual Life Space Crisis Intervention with an early-adolescent girl has been written by Bonnie McCarty and is reproduced in the Appendix. Of course, the full effectiveness of this method depends on competency-based training. Certification courses are available at sites in North America and overseas.

A TALE OF TWO SCHOOLS

Carol Dawson (2001, 2003) conducted an experimental study of student crises in two junior high school programs serving students with emotional disturbance.[9] These special education schools were both located in a large eastern-seaboard city. Students came from neighborhoods in which abuse, poverty, violence, gangs, and drugs were prevalent. The schools were located a few miles apart in fairly new facilities. Each served about 40 or so students with a staff of 17, including counselors, teachers, and paraprofessionals.

The schools had similar behavior management programs based on earning points and levels. Students who presented significant behavior problems were sent to staff in Crisis Resolution Rooms. The schools and students were similar in all respects except for the following:

- Experimental school staff received LSCI training as a solution strategy for crisis.

- Control school staff received support in developing their own solutions for crisis.

Dawson noted that prior research by the Council for Exceptional Children found that most special educators lacked formal training in working with students in crisis (Dawson, 2001, 2003). This was certainly true in both schools she studied, where about 90 percent of staff initially did not feel competent managing crises presented by students.

Crisis as Opportunity

In the experimental LSCI school, staff learned to use crisis situations as a time for teaching rather than punishment (Long & Morse, 1996). Interventions in times of crisis were designed to help students recognize their self-defeating thinking, feeling, and behaving; take responsibility for behavior; and develop constructive ways of responding.

This intervention targeted specific behaviors that got students in trouble. Following is an example of a typical intervention:

> Ann, age 11, was referred to the Crisis Resolution Room after a hostile verbal encounter with the school bus matron. Ann was furious, insisting the matron was picking on her. Staff de-escalated her anger and, when she was calm, explored in detail the bus incident as well as earlier events at her foster home. Her emotions changed from anger to grief as she poured out a tearful story about a phone call

received by her foster mother the night before. Ann's biological mother was moving to Florida with two of Ann's siblings, but not Ann. She felt abandoned, hurt, and angry. The
interviewer showed understanding of the difficult time Ann
must be having at this moment. The discussion helped Ann
realize she was not angry with the bus matron, who became
the displaced target of her frustration. Ann shared that she
seldom talks about problems from home but then becomes
so full of anger at school that she can't think clearly. A plan
was developed in which Ann would seek out staff and speak
about problems when she arrived at school rather than creating new problems. This solution was role-played until Ann
was comfortable. The teacher and counselor were informed
of the plan, and the counselor agreed to help Ann with
home issues. Ann was able to return to class.

Over a period of a year, data were gathered to compare
outcomes of the LSCI and control schools. Table 7.1 summarizes the significant positive student gains. The frequency of
crises and suspensions decreased in the LSCI experimental
school. Significant numbers of students were being main-
streamed and transferred to less restrictive settings. None were
sent to more restrictive settings. Students were more engaged
in school, as evidenced by attendance rates.

All staff who took LSCI training reported more confidence
in their ability to manage student crisis behavior. They found
this training helpful in understanding why the students
behaved as they once did. One paraprofessional commented, "I
used to be afraid of the students and not know what to say or
do. I was very quiet and avoided contact with them. Now I am
confident in my abilities. I find that every time I use Life Space
Crisis Intervention, I become closer to the students and now
they come to me when they have problems. It feels good to
make a difference in their lives."

In contrast, staff from the control group became increasingly exasperated by the "revolving door" of crisis situations.
When disruption continued, the philosophy frequently was
"students need more discipline," which took the form of phone
calls home, additional time out of the classroom, and more
punishment and alienation.

Table 7.1
A Year in the Life of Two Schools

	LSCI School	Control School
Frequency of student crisis compared with previous year	Decreased 56%	Increased 75%
Frequency of suspensions compared with previous year	Decreased 20%	Decreased 6%
Students transferring to less restrictive settings	27%	2%
Students transferring to more restrictive settings	0%	6%
Students mainstreamed	41%	9%
Average student attendance	86%	74%
Staff expressing confidence in ability to manage crises	All staff members	Two staff members

Several students at each school who had emotional outbursts resulting in removal from the classroom were interviewed at the end of the study. They were asked, "What do you need from teachers when you are most upset?" A student at the LSCI school replied, "Kids have a lot on their minds. Sometimes I can't think at school when I am upset. It helps to talk to teachers." In contrast, a youth at the control school answered, "Nothing. Teachers can't help me with my problems. I have to take care of myself."

Schools are required to provide positive behavior support in the least restrictive environment to special-needs students. However, educators who are not prepared to work with difficult students often employ management strategies that provoke power struggles and exacerbate the problem (Shores, Gunter, & Jack, 1993). Teachers commonly express concern that disruptive behavior results in lost teaching time, conflict with students, and low teacher morale (Malone, Bonitz, & Rickett, 1998). Traditional methods of detention, suspension, and expulsion may suppress behavior in the short term but are ineffective with students who exhibit chronic behavior problems (Gable, Quinn, Rutherford, Howell, & Hoffman, 1998).

These findings suggest that LSCI provides methods through which even troubled and troubling students can become "teachable." In Dawson's terms, LSCI operates like a "laser beam approach directed at the behaviors which violate school codes of conduct" (2001, p. 68). The focus is on identifying patterns of problems, discovering the reason for the behavior, and teaching the necessary skills to prevent recurrence of the problem behavior.

Asking the Right Questions

In seeking a solution to any problem, the answers we get depend on the questions we ask. For example, what would be the effect of asking each of these questions about a student with disruptive behavior?

- What consequences can we administer to stop this behavior?
- Why does this behavior persist in spite of negative consequences?

The first question triggers a search for tougher punishments. The second question focuses on figuring out what maintains this behavior so that more constructive coping strategies can be taught.

Many assume that "consequences" change destructive behavior, but often such punishment only motivates further resistance. For many reasons, administering negative consequences is not a very efficient or effective way of eliminating negative behavior or teaching positive behavior. Thus the new direction in education and treatment is to determine the function of the behavior and use this information to create positive intervention plans (Gable, Quinn, Rutherford, Howell, & Hoffman, 2000).

Schools are legally mandated to conduct "functional behavior assessments" with students showing serious problem behavior in order to discover the causes of these problems and develop positive behavioral interventions. However, educators often lack the knowledge to make effective assessments and develop appropriate interventions (Nelson, Roberts, Mathur, & Rutherford, 1999).

Life Space Crisis Intervention helps adults to disengage from punitive roles. Instead, staff are given practical skills to communicate with young people about the serious and self-defeating problems they present. This not only enlists youth in problem solving but also provides important new data about the meaning of troublesome behavior.

"NOW I GET RESPECT"

Andrew's Story

Andrew is a 10-year-old student who repeatedly threatened violence to peers in his elementary school. The principal reported that he wanted this boy out of his school: "He is just a troublemaker. He hits other kids, and he threatens that he is going to throw them off the bridge. I have already suspended him several times, and now I need to step up the consequences." Andrew's story provides an example of how staff who learn to understand the meaning of surface behavior are able to develop positive interventions.

After hearing the many dramatic reports about Andrew's threats of violence, one is surprised to meet this tiny, frail, pale boy dressed in army fatigues. Lacking the physical prowess to become a real bully, Andrew intimidates others with violent talk and threats:

> I like to beat kids up and take away their bikes. But if you say you're going to kill somebody, you get in trouble, so I just say something like "I'm going to barbecue your head." They know what I mean, but then if the principal asks me, I would just say, "That's silly. How could you barbecue a head?"

Andrew is fascinated with military metaphor and more than once has uttered the mantra "I must secure my person." He indicated that he is training his little brother to be able to stand up and protect himself as well. He appears depressed, and when asked if he worries about things, Andrew said, "Yes, I can't sleep at night. My head is going too much, so I sneak around the house."

It is reported that Andrew's father is unemployed and spends his time at home surfing the Web and playing violent video games. He often explodes in a violent temper. On one occasion when Andrew's mother was called to school, she slapped Andrew in the face. Although teachers suspect abuse, Andrew refuses to talk about anything personal concerning his family background.

Andrew gets very frustrated when he fails and often says something like, "I should just blow my brains out and kill myself." He has been preoccupied with death since kindergarten, when his grandmother died of cancer while living in his home. Andrew has nightmares and often reports not having slept the night before. When in a bad mood, he makes bizarre comments, such as that he knows how to strangle people with wire, which frighten his peers. They avoid him and seldom pick him for any games. It also seems clear that Andrew's teacher, like his peers, fears and dislikes him.

Andrew is glad that other kids are afraid of him. In his words, "Kids used to pick on me, but now I get respect." We asked him if he could remember when he was small and not able to fight back. He shared an incident that occurred in first grade, when older kids held him over the side of a bridge. He acknowledged that now he threatens to do this to other kids, although he has never done so.

"Can you remember when you decided to quit letting people pick on you?" we asked. He shared that in first grade someone stole his bike. Andrew recruited another youngster, found the boy who had Andrew's bike, beat him up until he cried, and then took the bike back. When asked, "Did you feel bad when he cried?" Andrew said, "No, I felt good. I like kids to be afraid of me. I do that a lot."

Figure 7.1 shows a "pathway to violence" compiled from aggression research. We used this model in discussions with

Figure 7.1
Pathway to Violence

Crisis	Brooding	Belligerence	Defiant Pride
Mistreatment	Seeks a solution	Oppositional	Aggression is rewarding
Traumatic Events	Coached in violence	Covert aggression	Hostile thinking and values
Emotional stress	Rejects victim role	Overt aggression	Antisocial peers, lifestyle

© Circle of Courage

Andrew to determine how far he had advanced along this problem pathway. Andrew was able to share concrete incidents about early mistreatment and the process by which he decided to hurt others so they would not hurt him. Here we summarize what was learned from this extended timeline:

Crisis. As a small child, Andrew experienced mistreatment from a violent father. Upon entering school, he was threatened by peers who held him over the side of a bridge. He also was traumatized by the death of his grandmother, who lived with his family. Andrew lived in terror both at school and at home.

Brooding. Andrew became a powerless victim searching for a solution. He was coached in violence by the model of a violent father and in his role as a victim of school bullying. Andrew recalls the specific instance when he quit being a victim and decided to fight back: "A bigger kid kept picking on me, but I couldn't fight him back. Then he stole my bike. I couldn't take it anymore."

Belligerence. Andrew described his first foray into violence in these words: "I got a friend who was strong, and we went and found the boy who took my bike. We beat him up and made him cry and got my bike back. After that, other kids were afraid of me and quit picking on me."

Defiant pride. Andrew's belligerence paid off. By the time he was 11, Andrew was a proud sword rattler. "All of the kids are scared of me," he said with clear satisfaction. A small, terrified kid learned how to frighten others away with outrageous verbal threats. He did this in a planned manner, carefully calibrating his threats so they would terrorize others without getting himself into too much trouble. In Andrew's terms, he had gained "respect."

On the basis of this LSCI with Andrew and other available information, we formed the hypothesis that Andrew's belligerent behavior is a protective reaction from a pervasive fear that he is not safe, that he will be hurt or even killed. His coping strategy is to frighten other people to keep himself safe. Of course, this leads to further hostility from peers and what approaches animosity from educators, who keep escalating consequences but are unable to change his pattern of behavior.

Andrew's case suggests how interview information can be used to conduct a functional behavior assessment. The purpose of a functional behavior assessment is to determine the meaning, intent, or goal behind a specific pattern of problem behavior. A functional assessment identifies events that trigger behavior as well as consequences that maintain behavior. Following is a brief outline of a process for conducting a functional assessment using Andrew's case as an example.

1. *Identify and define the problem.* Behavior should be described in very specific terms. The principal who said Andrew was disruptive and a troublemaker contributes little to understanding this behavior. By stating that Andrew makes specific threats to hurt or kill others and himself, the behavior is clearly defined.

2. *Gather information on the possible intent of the behavior.* Under what circumstances does this problem occur? Andrew's case involves reports from various people who observed his behavior. However, without Andrew's own account of his preoccupation with danger ("I must secure my person"), it would be hard to make sense of his threats. The team hypothesized that Andrew's problem behavior was a response to a perceived threat of hostility and fear of harm or death.

3. *Develop a positive behavior intervention plan.* The hypothesis that emerged was that Andrew's behavior was triggered by fear and had the goal of providing protection. The team decided to change his placement to a different school and classroom, where he would likely feel safe and accepted by the principal, teacher, and peers. The IEP committee believed that Andrew might succeed if he could be placed in a nurturing classroom environment.

He was transferred to another public school, where his likable qualities were apparent to his new teacher. When Andrew's behavior was inappropriate, this would be handled in a benign, supportive, and instructional manner rather than in escalating confrontation and consequences, as was the case in his previous school.

4. *Evaluate the intervention's effectiveness.* A team including the principal, teacher, Andrew, and his mother met periodically to review his progress in the new setting. In fact, the pattern of behavior that had characterized his earlier placement was no longer seen, and there have been no further threats. Andrew loves his new teacher and classmates, and they reciprocate his positive behavior.

Simply because of his problem behavior, Andrew might well have been placed in a segregated school for students with behavior disorders or perhaps in a highly restrictive program designed to "discipline" delinquents. When the basis of his behavior was identified, an entirely different solution was devised. In his current classroom, with positive support and opportunities to resolve conflicts in a respectful manner, Andrew continues to thrive. Although it is uncertain what may be happening at home, for Andrew, school has become a safe harbor in a stormy world.

NOTES

[1] Reproduced with permission from Wolff, T. (1989). *This Boy's Life: A Memoir.* New York: Atlantic Monthly Press, pp. 250–252. Tobias Wolff is a professor at Stanford University. *This Boy's Life* is also a movie starring Leonardo diCaprio.

[2] These ideas are applications of principles derived from research on angry conflict reviewed by Zillman (1993) and clinical strategies for managing conflict cycles by Long and Morse (1996).

[3] The most widely researched crisis prevention models are Nonviolent Crisis Intervention® by the Crisis Prevention Institute, Brookfield, Wisconsin, and Therapeutic Crisis Intervention by Cornell University, Ithaca, New York.

[4] This therapeutic strategy was first called the Life Space Interview by Fritz Redl and David Wineman in their book *The Aggressive Child*

(1957). Their model was refined at the University of Michigan and the National Institute of Mental Health by Nicholas Long and William Morse (1996), co-authors of *Conflict in the Classroom*. It was renamed Life Space Crisis Intervention by Long, Wood, and Fecser (2001). The journal *Reclaiming Children and Youth,* which is edited by Nicholas Long and Larry Brendtro, carries a regular feature on developing skills for LSCI.

[5] Information on training in Life Space Therapy methods is available at **www.reclaiming.com**. For a complete list of senior trainers and national training sites, contact the Life Space Crisis Intervention Institute, 226 Landis Rd., Hagerstown, MD 21704.

[6] In a large urban school district, counselors, psychologists, social workers, and special educators certified in LSCI documented 100 crisis interventions. In the great majority of cases, staff used strategies of de-escalation and securing timelines of what happened. In half the cases, this led to a diagnosis of the central issue. Each of the next three interventions was employed with successively less frequency. Although not all students needed the complete LSCI, the limited use of the more intensive clinical strategies was assumed to be related to tight time schedules in school settings and the need for more sophisticated staff clinical skills (Long, Fecser, & Brendtro, 1998).

[7] Long, Wood, and Fecser (2001) describe additional specific reclaiming interventions for each of these six problems. These are tied to specific staff competencies that constitute the training curriculum for LSCI.

[8] The most prominent social skills curriculum is the *Skillstreaming* series (Goldstein & McGinnis, 1997). Other extensively researched social skills programs include the *Girls and Boys Town Social Skills Curriculum,* available from Girls and Boys Town Press, Omaha, Nebraska, and *The Prepare Curriculum,* published by Research Press, Champaign, Illinois.

[9] This discussion summarizes the findings from a dissertation Carol A. Dawson (2001) completed for her doctoral degree at Nova Southeastern University.

CHAPTER EIGHT

The Developmental Audit

When an airplane crashes, an elaborate system is used to evaluate the cause of the disaster and to prevent future recurrences. But when a kid "crashes," there is no established system for determining the nature of the problem so that appropriate corrective action can be taken. The Developmental Audit[1] addresses the need for strength-based planning with youth in conflict. The goal is to identify a young person's problems and potentials in order to develop plans to foster positive growth and development. A core assumption is that the best expert on a youth's life is a young person who has lived it.

THE UNTAPPED EXPERTS

Anna Freud once told therapists that if they did not understand something, perhaps they should ask the children. Listening to the voice of children was a theme espoused by early youth work pioneers committed to democratic principles of involving young citizens in decision making. In the 1920s, Janusz Korczak designed his school for street children as a miniature democracy in which children were given responsibilities in developing and administering rules that governed their behavior. Lawrence Kohlberg called Korczak's children's court the prototype of the just community school (Brendtro & Hinders, 1990). By 1928, Coral Liepmann of Germany was able to publish an extensive international study of programs for children in trouble that employed principles of self-governance.

The wisdom of listening to youth was largely forgotten as "professionalized" treatment models became adult dominated. By the end of the 20th century, researchers would describe most programs for children with emotional and behavior disorders as "curriculums of control" (Knitzer, Steinberg, & Fleisch, 1990). In a study of school dropouts, Fine (1991) found that students were systematically silenced and excluded from significant input in their own education. Students report that most adults do not really listen to them. A typical comment is "Why do they ask for our opinion when they are going to tell us that their way is the right way?" (p. 45). Some adults make token gestures toward youth involvement while continuing a process of adult domination. For example, one alternative school for youth at risk invites students to attend meetings of the interdisciplinary teams involved in developing intervention plans. The student is then boxed into signing a written contract of behavioral expectations, with provisions crafted in advance to assure the adults' desired control outcomes.

Youth with problems are often seen as immature and irresponsible, and professionals seldom involve them in planning the services they are to receive. Gabor and Greene (1991) interviewed teens in out-of-home placement to determine if they were involved in planning for their future. Among 36 youths in the study, none recalled having been consulted in designing the case plan. Half were not even provided with significant information about the placements they were given. Their responses conveyed feelings of helplessness in the face of dominating adults. The researchers concluded,

> Young people have their own views and opinions about
> their situation and about the services they are receiving.
> They will share these views if given encouragement and
> the opportunity. If the services provided to young people
> are to be of real assistance to them, those closest to
> them . . . must ensure that young people are provided the
> opportunity to express their views and that, when they do,
> someone is listening! (Gabor & Greene, 1991, p. 18)

Because youth are the only ones with an inside track on the goals of their behavior, it is puzzling that this data source has so often been ignored. Some researchers have argued that "deviant individuals" make unreliable informants (Loeber, 1991). Perhaps, but scientists are truth detectors. Even the fact that a youth chooses to lie raises intriguing hypotheses and opportunities for communication. Has a trusted adult betrayed the young person? Does he fear punishment for being honest? Is she embarrassed to disclose a painful or shameful event? When a youth feels it is safe to share, the need to deceive diminishes. But no person is an open book, and we all need to preserve some areas of personal privacy. The stories we dare to share depend on how we decide between "what is true and what is tellable" (Spence, 1984, p. 62).

Perhaps the most important assessment is conducted not by the adult but by the youth. Canadian research found that youth will not cooperate with workers with whom they have no established connections. Nor will they respond to intrusive assessments that pose irrelevant or demeaning questions about their personal lives, relationships, and activities (Artz, Nicholson, Halsall, & Larke, 2001). As long as the young person remains "the missing team member," youth are likely to resist or sabotage plans foisted on them (Brendtro & Bacon, 1995).

A former youth in care, Brian Raychaba (1990) observed that youth are the best experts on their own lives but are often deprived of a significant voice in matters affecting them. A climate of mutual distrust will have to be replaced with honest dialogue and shared decision making. This new climate calls for a fresh approach to assessment. Adult expertise must be used to involve the youth in defining the problem and searching for solutions (Clark, 2001).

DECODING PROBLEM BEHAVIOR

No conduct is peculiar when it is understood. It is only the misunderstood child who seems peculiar.

—John Morgan (1936, p. 91)

The Developmental Audit provides a comprehensive means of assessment and treatment planning that incorporates the private logic and goals of the youth.[2] Life Space Therapy methods are used to provide data for assessment and treatment planning. Through an alliance with a youth, one gains access to the private logic and personal goals underlying the youth's behavior. Additional perspectives from family, teachers, peers, and others in the child's ecology round out the picture of the child's situation. As with a financial audit, assets and liabilities both are inventoried. This strength-based process yields fresh insights not obtainable by deficit-based assessments.

Because it is based on the universal needs of children, the Developmental Audit applies to a variety of settings and a range of problems. Schools, courts, treatment professionals, and families require solid information before making appropriate decisions about youth with challenging behavior. The Developmental Audit is critical when a potentially life-altering decision is to be made about a young person's future. It is also used for ongoing growth planning in programs that rely on strength-based principles. The following are examples of situations in which the Developmental Audit has been useful:

Precipitous problems erupt with little warning or escalate previous problems. Behavior crosses the boundary of what is tolerated in a given setting. These youth may be at risk for more intrusive interventions, such as removal from school or transfer to alternative education, treatment, or the juvenile or criminal justice system. For example, Christi's parents sought a Developmental Audit after repeated home and school truancies and substance abuse threatened her removal from the family and expulsion from school.

Chronic problems persist in spite of repeated interventions and escalating consequences. Such behaviors continue unabated or intensify as the youth exhausts a string of programs and placements. Typically, a thick case file documents costly failed interventions by multiple professionals and systems. For example, Jared was removed from his fifth foster home because of unexplained depression and oppositional behavior.

Ongoing assessment with the Developmental Audit balances problems with potentials to develop proactive growth plans. The Developmental Audit is consistent with research-validated best practices that are ecological and need-based (Kemp, Whittaker, & Tracy, 1997). The Developmental Audit is used to plan interventions fostering resilience and positive youth development. Schools use Developmental Audits to comply with IDEA 97 requirements for IEP or functional assessments of behavior. Courts use Developmental Audits to develop appropriate dispositions for delinquent and mal-treated youth. Treatment programs use Developmental Audits for developing strength-based interventions with children and families.

The Developmental Audit identifies the private logic and coping strategies underlying a youth's adaptive and self-defeating behavior. The Developmental Audit is based on collaboration with the youth and others who know the youth well. The young person is enlisted in exploring significant life events. First priority is given to conflicts and crises the youth currently faces, although this often leads to other unresolved issues.

Because the Developmental Audit takes an ecological perspective, families and others working directly in the child's life space can play an important role. Parents of children in conflict have commonly felt excluded from the evaluation. Too often they have been seen as the cause of the problem and not part of the solution. Even sophisticated mental health programs may treat parents of children in conflict as patients rather than partners. In similar fashion, the assumption that "parent education" is the solution may be unintentionally patronizing to many parents who have worked for years to become experts on the problems of their youngsters. Even if parenting has been less than adequate, family members are still the only lifelong experts when it comes to the child in question. One mother with a history of depression and alcoholism said, "I know everybody thinks I have been a lousy parent, but I have been watching over my girl for 12 years, and I know more about her and care more about her than anybody on this earth." In many cases, families can use the Developmental Audit to finally get to the bottom of problems of long duration.

In settings where a formal functional assessment of behavior is needed, the Developmental Audit can serve this purpose. Typically, a functional assessment involves defining the problem behavior, collecting historical and background data, and observing behavior. In addition, the Developmental Audit uses Life Space Therapy interview methods so that the youth's private logic and goals become a primary data source. After this information is integrated, a hypothesis about the meaning of the behavior is formed and used to create a positive intervention.

The scope of the Developmental Audit will vary, depending on the type of problem and the use to be made of the recommendations. Some Developmental Audits are streamlined in recognition of limited resources. Thus a functional analysis of behavior should not produce an "elegant behavioral support plan" that far exceeds the "skills, time, resources, and administrative support available in schools" (Sugai & Lewis, 1999, p. 20). On the other hand, when a juvenile court requests a Developmental Audit for use in considering the possible transfer of a youth into the adult system, the report must be sufficiently thorough to withstand cross-examination. Typically, these more intensive Developmental Audits are produced by a team and may involve a dozen or more hours of direct contact with youth and significant others.

Information gathered from youth is not meant to eliminate educational, psychological, or psychiatric evaluations; multiple data sources provide a stronger foundation for diagnosis and planning. As strength-based assessment instruments become more available, these tools can help enhance the Developmental Audit.[3] If other specialized evaluation is required (e.g., violence classification in corrections, assessment for substance abuse treatment), the Developmental Audit still provides an umbrella of information essential for growth planning. By focusing on information that is potentially most important, it helps make sense out of a mass of potentially misleading material, including reams of irrelevant or pessimistic commentary that clutter many case files.

CONSTRUCTING GROWTH PLANS

The Developmental Audit draws information related to Connections, Continuity, Dignity, and Opportunity (CCDO). These principles are grounded in resilience science and positive youth development (Seita, Mitchell, & Tobin, 1996; Seita & Brendtro, 2002). The Developmental Audit seeks answers to questions in these four domains.

Connections: What *social supports* in the child's life space can enhance positive growth?

Continuity: What *coping patterns* will guide the child on pathways of positive growth?

Dignity: What *personal strengths* help the child meet needs and attain positive growth?

Opportunity: What *growth plans* can be created as adults and the young person work in an alliance?

Two major impediments to valid assessment are a lack of relevant data and an overabundance of irrelevant data. The CCDO model helps make sense out of the confusing array of possible information. It is sufficiently broad in scope to be comprehensive, and yet it keeps the focus on factors most crucial to positive growth and development.

The CCDO model provides landmarks for conducting a Developmental Audit to produce a growth plan. We do not prescribe a standard list of questions for interrogation, for it has been shown to foster resistance and block communication. Instead, these categories are more like "talking points" for exploring with young people the significant challenges in their lives. Alfred Adler once developed an extensive questionnaire intended to evoke what adults might want to learn about children, and then cautioned never to let this list interfere with the spontaneity of communication.

Here we briefly describe how each of the four broad CCDO questions is addressed in a Developmental Audit.

Connections: Social Supports

The life space of childhood consists of connections to home, school, peers, and community. We seek to take a brief inventory of possible sources of support as well as conflicts that may create discord in the child's life. Using the Connections form (Figure 8.1), we ask the young person to briefly scan his or her "connections" with family, peers, school, and the community. Like a radio scanning stations in search of something interesting, we are checking the ecology in which the student lives. This is not a flaw-finding expedition but a positive process that helps us better know this child.

Starting with the *family quadrant,* we might note where the student lives, who her caregivers and siblings are, and perhaps what she enjoys doing with family members. For example, one student reported that she spends most of her free time caring for her ailing grandmother. In the *peers quadrant,* we learn a bit about favorite friends and what they like to do together. Perhaps we might inquire about what her parents think about these companions. In the *school quadrant,* we can jot down favorite subjects or activities and get a glimpse of how closely she is bonded to school and teachers. In the *community quadrant,* we note other outside connections, such as jobs, clubs, church youth groups, or a relationship with a mentor or counselor. It is also important to understand the racial and cultural connections of a youth, which can have a strong impact on values and relationships. As we show genuine interest in the players and activities in the youth's life, trust is advanced.

Being aware of major supports and stressors in a child's life space enables adults to be supportive even when external events are beyond their realm of influence. By scanning the child's connections to the community ecology, we are also better equipped to decode the meaning of the child's behavior. It is also useful to have family members offer additional perspectives on the connections that they believe are important in the life of their child.

Figure 8.1
Connections

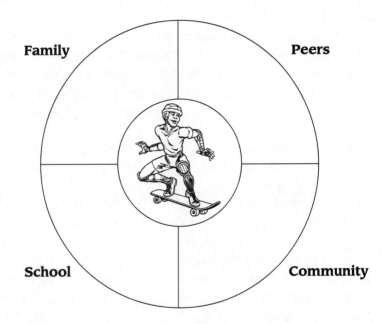

Continuity: Coping Patterns

Our most challenging children travel through life along self-defeating pathways. To understand and change these patterns, we seek to make sense of their behavior. The focus of behavior assessment is the *timeline* of significant life events. Timelines are widely used for interpreting the meaning of behavior. Detectives build timelines to deduce "whodunit." Therapists use timelines for tracking origins of symptom behavior. Functional behavioral assessments use an "ABC" timeline to demonstrate how antecedents lead to behavior, which leads to consequences.

The Developmental Audit uses the strategies of Life Space Crisis Intervention, discussed in Chapter 7, to identify the timelines of sentinel events in a child's life. These are usually situations that were charged with positive or negative emotions and thus are likely to influence future behavior, as shown in Figure 8.2.

Timelines are particularly useful for helping children who do not think in a logical, sequential fashion to sort out their behavior. For example, suppose a student says, "The teacher kicked me out of class because he hates me!" We would construct a *behavior incident timeline* to help the youth check private logic against reality. We would simply track the sequence of events surrounding the student's getting kicked out of class. Sometimes it is helpful to follow an actual line drawn on a piece of paper to clarify the sequence of events. The discussion would have a tone of "Can you help me understand what happened?" The adult must remain very supportive so the youth can keep calm and think clearly. A particularly useful behavior incident timeline is the Conflict Cycle, discussed in Chapter 2. As opposed to a linear presentation, this one enables the youth to see how events escalate. Other cyclical timelines that may be useful with certain youth have been developed in the fields of substance abuse and sexual offending.

It is not essential to draw timelines on paper, but doing so helps many youths become more involved in this concrete presentation. Visualizing a timeline helps them to better understand a complex sequence of events. Timelines track not

Figure 8.2
Critical Life Events

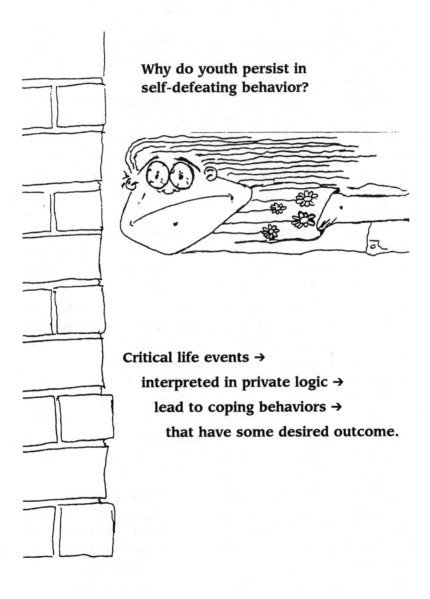

**Why do youth persist in
self-defeating behavior?**

Critical life events →

interpreted in private logic →

lead to coping behaviors →

that have some desired outcome.

only behavioral events but also feelings and private logic. Timelines enable us to identify common thinking errors such as self-centered thinking, blaming others, assuming the worst, and minimizing one's behavior (Gibbs, Potter, Goldstein, & Brendtro, 1998).

Expanded timelines give students a bigger picture of their behavior. For example, we can map a multiple-year timeline on which a student identifies the ages at which various problems arose. A student who has been in many schools can help organize this educational history in a timeline. Students who have gone through multiple placements can try to make sense out of their transient existence. Once trust has developed, students are able to examine timelines of abuse, substance abuse, or delinquency that help track behavioral pathways.

Research in developmental psychopathology shows that certain youths follow predictable *problem pathways,* which also can be tracked with timelines. In Chapter 7 we saw how a timeline of Andrew's trajectory of violence was used to interpret the meaning of his behavior. He was following a pathway of overt aggression; other children may employ covert or passive-aggressive strategies (Loeber & Farrington, 1998). Youth may also follow pathways of hedonistic, risk-taking behavior. Children who internalize their problems may travel pathways of retreat leading to substance abuse, depression, and hopelessness (Larson & Brendtro, 2000). Identifying patterns and pathways of coping behavior enables a youth to examine past choices and consider reversing negative trajectories.

Timelines presented on paper can provide a useful tool for record keeping and treatment planning. A recurring complaint of educators and treatment staff is the massive overload of paperwork that diverts them from direct work with children. The unique aspect of timeline forms is that they can be completed as a natural by-product of conversations with students. The timeline sheet becomes an instrument of authentic assessment produced jointly by student and facilitator. It chronicles not just a problem but a problem-solving process.[4]

Dignity: Strengths and Needs

Providing children with dignity means celebrating their worth, cultivating their strengths, and attending to their unmet needs. Only children treated with respect are able to develop respect for self and others. Children and youth deprived of dignity respond with indignation or hopelessness. Dignity and respect are absent from relationships between challenging children and coercive adults (Curwin & Mendler, 1999). To experience dignity and self-worth, young people must develop their personal potentials and believe they are of value to others. Toward this end, the Developmental Audit includes the strengths and needs of the youth.

Those working with challenging youth are often frustrated in their attempts to provide guidance or penetrate protective shells. Larson and Van Paten (2000) train mentors to reach these youth by identifying unmet needs:

> Hard-to-reach youth or at-risk youth are not open enough to allow this information or us into their life. In a sense, they have "shut the window" so we cannot see in or talk to them about life. The "window" into their life is in knowing their felt needs. (p. 5)

Specifically, the mentor engages a young person in discussing the personal challenges the youth faces in developing *trust, talent, responsibility,* and *respect.* Figure 8.3 on page 172 replicates Abraham Maslow's (1954) pyramid portrayal of growth needs. It should be noted that these dimensions are direct expressions of the Circle of Courage resilience code.[5]

Because these four growth needs are foundations of positive development, the Developmental Audit includes data from the youth and informants on these critical dimensions.

Trust is a prerequisite to belonging. It is also the foundation for other levels of the pyramid. A professional may recognize that a child has problems with trust, yet can easily misjudge whether he or she has built a trusting alliance with the young person (Safran & Muran, 2000). Young people who are "veterans" of counseling learn many strategies to keep helpers at bay (Duncan, Hubble, & Miller, 1997). To begin talking with youth

Figure 8.3
Dignity

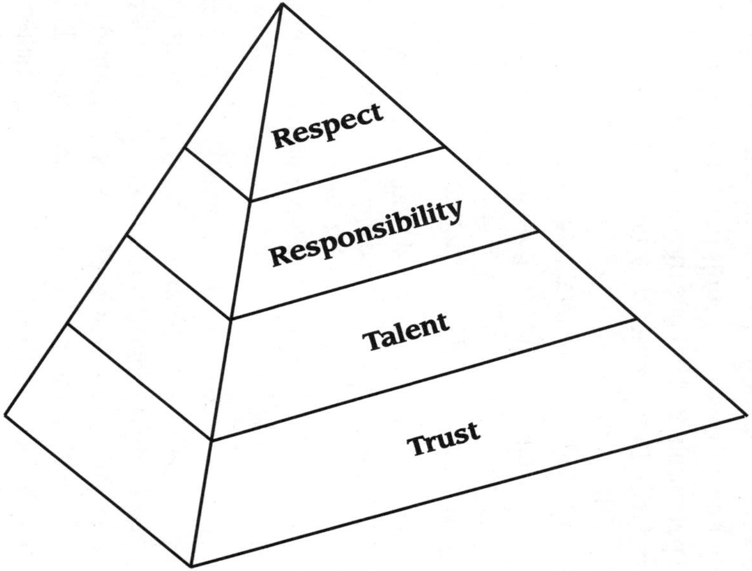

Respect

Responsibility

Talent

Trust

about trust requires that the adult project some level of comfort and trust, even in the presence of antagonism. In his classic book *Wayward Youth,* August Aichhorn (1935) described how, from the first encounter, he carefully constructed a basis for trust with youth who viewed adults as enemies:

> If a child is in open conflict and expecting an attack, he is disappointed. I do not ask him what he has done, I do not press him to tell me what has happened and in contrast to the police or the juvenile court, I do not try to pry out of him information which he is unwilling to give. In many cases where I feel the child wants to be questioned so that he can come into opposition with me, I say that he may hold back whatever information he wishes; that I understand that one does not want to tell everything to a person one has met for the first time. When I add that I would do likewise he is usually willing to fall into a conversation with me about something remote from his difficulties but in line with his interests. . . . He feels, rather than understands, that I am not an authority with whom he must fight but an understanding ally. (p. 129)

When we ask youth in conflict whom they trust, many answer with the blunt assertion "Nobody!" Although many youths are very loyal to peers, they are often bound together by questionable activities. One girl said she had only one real friend; the basis of their trust was using illegal drugs and having bulimia purging contests together. On the other hand, often a youth can point to a trusted relative, mentor, or peer who is a positive force in his or her life. One sexually abused boy who experienced two failed adoptions after leaving a Romanian orphanage said his youth pastor was the only person in the world he could trust. Even by discussing trust and distrust, youth take the first step on the road to recognizing their need for others. Here are examples of private logic related to trust and distrust:[6]

- "When I'm feeling down, I have people who care about me."
- "If you trust someone, they'll probably just stab you in the back."

- "Sometimes I feel all alone in this world."

Talent is the basis of mastery. Although we begin by accepting youth in spite of their inadequacies, an early goal is to instill competence and mastery. Adults become talent scouts helping youth discover and cultivate their potential.

Some youth feel devoid of talent or are very self-conscious about stating any positives they might have. Their lack of motivation often indicates an unwillingness to risk failure. Others are confident or even arrogant about their abilities. Youth and adults may value very different talents. One youth turned his problems into virtues, telling us, "I hate school but I am street smart. I can read danger and defend myself." Because talents are often hidden, adults conduct "talent hunts" for lost potentials. One young teen girl said, "I used to be real smart until second grade, but then I had a bad teacher and turned dumb."

Asking youth what they like to do in their free time can unearth unsuspected potentials. A seemingly unmotivated student suddenly became animated when he could talk about repairing cars. Such interests may be tickets to untapped talents. Reports from parents and other significant adults may offer additional clues. The following comments are representative of the private logic of young people regarding their talent and ability:

- "I am pretty good at solving difficult problems."

- "Growing up, I felt I couldn't do anything right."

- "I stick with what I know instead of trying new things and failing."

Responsibility involves making decisions to shape the course of one's life by exercising self-control and independence. Resilient people believe they are in control of their destiny rather than helpless pawns of others. The "will to power" is a normal need that is fulfilled by autonomy and "self efficacy" (Bandura, 1995).

Problems with irresponsible use of power wreck human relationships. Some youth are terrified by the power of angry adults who control their lives. Others wield coercive power themselves or project defiant power: "Nobody tells me what to do." Beneath the bluster, one often finds a youth who feels powerless. Some angry and impulsive youths are afraid of their power: "When I lose my temper, I go wild and nobody can control me." At the extreme are young people who feel totally helpless and unable to control their lives. This sense of helplessness is related to depression. The ultimate loss of control comes when a person can no longer compensate for stress and retreats into psychosis. Following are examples of the private logic of youth in relation to responsible power:

- "I have a lot of goals for my life."

- "My future seems too much out of my control."

- "No matter how hard I try, things don't work out the way I want them to."

Respect involves treating others as we wish to be treated, to relate to others in a spirit of generosity. It is the core of all cultures. Humans are altruistic beings who experience a genuine sense of worth only by being of some value to others. Without respect, life loses its meaning.

In his study *The Spiritual Life of Children*, Harvard psychiatrist Robert Coles (1990) observes that crisis prompts a child to ponder intensely his or her past life, present state, and future. At such times, spiritual questions come to the fore. There is growing recognition even in secular schools and agencies that youth need opportunities to talk about such matters of the heart (Kessler, 2000; Lantieri, 2001; Richards & Bergin, 1997). In fact, many youths are eager to talk about these issues if the adult can make such communication safe. Coles found fifth graders amazingly responsive to the question "Tell me, as best you can, who you are—what about you matters most, what makes you the person you are" (1990, p. 308). Here are some examples of the private logic of youth concerning the purpose or meaninglessness of life:

- "It's important to help people, even if they don't deserve it."

- "Growing up, I often felt like nothing really mattered."

- "A lot of times I feel there is no real meaning in my life."

Trust, talent, responsibility, and respect are at the heart of living in harmony and balance. Yet these are not the topics many youths have an opportunity to discuss with adults. Young people who can share their dreams and doubts open a window to their soul and allow adults to validate their worth and dignity.

Opportunity: Goals for Growth

The final stage of the Developmental Audit is to develop a plan for growth. Data gathered on connections, continuity, and dignity provide the basis for opportunity, the development of positive interventions. Studies by the Search Institute have shown that the ability of youth to overcome risk is a function of external supports as well as internal strengths and resilience (Benson, 1997). The Developmental Audit has uncovered potential assets as well as problems and unmet needs. It has inventoried a youth's social supports, coping patterns, and personal strengths.

Plans that are imposed on young people cannot be expected to foster positive change. Thus the development of growth plans should entail more than lip-service involvement of youth and family, who must be seen not just as *consumers of services* but also as *creators of solutions.* The core definition of strength-based intervention is reinforcing child and family assets rather than focusing on deficits (Laursen, 2000). Thus educators or helping practitioners take on the role of co-planners rather than prescriptive experts.

Webster's defines *opportunity* as a condition favorable for the attainment of goals. We provide opportunity by helping a young person meet needs, overcome difficulties, and develop strengths. Figure 8.4 is a guide for formulating growth plans. The first column of the planning guide identifies four universal *growth needs* of children with examples of related behaviors. The second column lists various problem behaviors that are seen when these *needs are frustrated.* The final column lists *goals for growth* anchored in the Circle of Courage. A completed growth plan identifies specific ways to provide opportunity for Belonging, Mastery, Independence, and Generosity. These goals mark the pathway to positive development.

Figure 8.4

Planning for Growth

Growth Needs	Needs Frustrated	Goals for Growth
Attachment	**Alienation**	**Belonging**
Trust	Distrust	a.
Warmth	Detachment	
Friendship	Rejection	b.
Cooperation	Antagonism	
Acceptance	Exclusion	c.
Achievement	**Incompetence**	**Mastery**
Talent	Inadequacy	a.
Concentration	Disinterest	
Comprehension	Confusion	b.
Organization	Chaos	
Coping	Defeat	c.
Autonomy	**Irresponsibility**	**Independence**
Responsibility	Undependability	a.
Assertiveness	Easily misled	
Self-confidence	Self-doubt	b.
Self-control	Recklessness	
Optimism	Helplessness	c.
Altruism	**Selfishness**	**Generosity**
Respect	Disrespect	a.
Kindness	Indifference	
Empathy	Rancor	b.
Forgiveness	Vengeance	
Purpose	Emptiness	c.

© Circle of Courage

"TRAVELING A NEW PATHWAY"
Craig's Story

Craig had been in out-of-home placements since age 10 and, with each new abandonment, became more angry and defiant. He would provoke adults, and most responded with counter-aggression. One private school put him in a phone booth–sized box for hours on end in futile power struggles. At age 11, he was placed in a punitive boot camp with adolescent offenders. Although he refuses to discuss it, Craig was sexually abused by these older youth.

When Craig returned to public school at age 12, he entered a new class and intentionally defied the teacher even before the bell had rung. Because he made various verbal threats to peers, Craig was suspended from school for 10 days. Midway into his suspension, Craig came in for a meeting for preplanning to develop a report for school and court staff. Initially, Craig thought the purpose of this meeting was to build a case to kick him out. Given past experience, that was a realistic best bet of adult intentions, and he entered with belligerence and distrust:

> This is a waste of time! I hate counselors. I have seen
> 20 of these "mind-benders." I never tell them shit,
> because they make up lies about me. None of them
> could figure me out but I figured them out. Adults are so
> stupid. I can tell just how they will act. They're so pre-
> dictable. This is boring. When can I leave?

Instead of reacting to his resistance, Natalie, his counselor, joined with it. She said, "You sure are good at figuring out and fighting adults, and you must have pretty good reasons. Since you won't let them find out anything about you, that means you are the only real expert on you. We have to come up with a report for the court and school, so it will be very important to get your ideas about what should happen to you. Nobody likes to be lied about, so we would like you to help us make sure absolutely every line makes sense to you."

In spite of periodic protests that "this is boring," Craig seemed intrigued with going over timelines of his life. He identified what he thought were the most rewarding and difficult things he had encountered. When Craig discovered that Natalie was respectful instead of judgmental, his need for combat diminished. Craig communicated for the rest of the morning, lapping up attention from two adults, his sarcasm alternating with longer interludes of humor and warmth.

Later that week, Craig and Natalie sat down at a word processor to co-produce the Developmental Audit. She had a draft, which they went over line by line. Craig was invited to challenge anything that didn't make sense to him, and if they couldn't agree, both viewpoints would be included. In actuality, consensus was reached on all information. Craig offered details not previously known and openly discussed problems that in other contexts would trigger defensiveness.

The Developmental Audit that Natalie created with Craig is reproduced here, beginning on page 180.[7] It uses the following straightforward format:

1. Presenting Problem

2. Significant Life Events

3. Supports and Strengths

4. Private Logic and Coping Strategies

5. Goals for Growth

This report is not a prototype of perfection, but an effort by a young professional who struggles daily with highly challenging students. Just two years ago, Natalie and colleagues were locked in constant power struggles with youth. Now they have real power, that which comes from a respectful alliance.

DEVELOPMENTAL AUDIT AND GROWTH PLAN
Columbia School District

STUDENT: Mr. Craig Wilson   GRADE: 8
REPORTER: Mrs. Natalie Compton, Behavior Specialist
TEACHER: Mrs. Joy Renz

PRESENTING PROBLEM

Craig is enrolled at Columbia Middle School in a self-contained special education class for emotionally disturbed children. He was referred for evaluation after an altercation with a male peer during which he allegedly said, "Don't mess with me because I know where to get a gun." Craig is serving a 10-day suspension while the IEP team reviews his placement.

SIGNIFICANT LIFE EVENTS

Craig is a pleasant-appearing and friendly 13-year-old who has recently moved to Columbia with his mother from Texas. School records indicate that Craig was identified as academically gifted in second grade and received differentiated instruction in reading and language arts in elementary school. Craig continues to achieve in about the 96th percentile and scores in the Superior Range on the WISC-III intelligence test.

Craig became eligible for special education services in fifth grade as a student with Serious Emotional Disturbance. He has diagnoses of ADHD and Oppositional Defiant Disorder and currently takes Zoloft and Dexedrine daily. Craig has had 10 educational placements, including a hospital-school, day treatment, and various public school settings. He also was in two private residential placements for youth with behavior disorders, but records are not available. He has previously been in therapy, and his psychiatric report is on file.

The Wilsons divorced when Craig was 10, and he lived with his father for a year. He was placed in a military school but was expelled for defiant behavior. Both parents had difficulty managing him, and he was placed in a series of mental health and treatment settings. His mother believes Craig experienced sexual abuse in one residential placement, but Craig will not discuss this. The parents had frequent custody battles, and Craig is currently in the care of his mother. He was released from a private Arizona boot camp earlier this year and returned home extremely angry and volatile. Craig briefly attended a private school and then was homeschooled by his mother, which only added to the stress in his relationships. Craig was placed on probation with the juvenile court after arrest for theft and threatening a peer in the neighborhood with an unloaded BB gun.

SUPPORTS AND STRENGTHS

Craig's strongest support is from his mother; he has little contact with his father. Although new to the community, Craig has made a few friends but has not yet been involved in activities outside of school. His strongest relationship in school is with his special education teacher. Craig is also seen regularly by his court services worker and is cooperative in that interaction.

Craig has many strengths and interests. They are listed here.

Strengths	Interests
Creative	Outdoor work
Can be polite	Animals
Intelligent	Canoeing
Good "debater"	Biking
Mature in many ways	Skiing
Likes to help others	Soccer
Compliments others	Computers
Excellent writer	Nintendo
Kindhearted to animals	Camping
Cares about his circle of friends	Ropes courses
Can do humorous imitations	
Wants to manage angry feelings	

PRIVATE LOGIC AND COPING STRATEGIES

Since early childhood, Craig has experienced turmoil, abandonment, and traumatic events and has lacked a consistent, supportive environment. In some of the many temporary placements, he learned to use inappropriate language and threatening behaviors for coping. He sees the world as an unpredictable place where adults are not to be trusted and others try to control him. He thinks people are making things up about him.

Raised in conflict at home and experiencing violence in institutions, Craig never accepted the victim role. To have some control, he became belligerent, oppositional, and covertly aggressive. His style has been to use sarcasm and pranks and to manipulate situations and people. In the past, he has distrusted counselors and psychologists, and he is proud that "they can't figure him out." He says, "I keep my shield up." Craig doesn't share what is bothering him and guards his true feelings, even in his family. Craig doesn't like to discuss his problems, so he makes excuses, blames others, or withdraws and shuts down, refusing to talk. Yet emotional stress triggers feelings of fear, rage, shame, and concern about additional abandonment—feelings that need to be dealt with. Craig does not feel secure, and he is not sure whether he will be placed in a correctional setting or moved to the noncustodial parent. He wonders if he will be welcome in school.

Craig initially tried to cope with the Columbia Middle School environment by cultivating an image of himself as a hostile, angry, tough guy, a strategy that worked in the past. Described as a "reactor," he has not been an "initiator" of violence. He sought status with others by talking about guns, making threats, and using profanity. As he gets older, he is beginning to see how he can cause huge problems with his comments in a public school. It is difficult to trust peers and make friends. He hears other students talking about him, and he sort of likes it that people are scared of him. He sometimes wears military fatigues and says his nickname in an earlier peer group was "Death-Raider." He has made some friends in his new school. He has a girlfriend he trusts and confides in and talks to as much as he can. He is considerate of and cares about his circle of friends.

Craig is experiencing some academic success. People recognize his intelligence and creative abilities. He helps others become successful academically, and he is beginning to create an image of himself as a person with many talents.

GOALS FOR GROWTH

Belonging: Craig's biggest challenge will be to find some adults he can trust. Having experienced repeated disruption in his school life and within his family, Craig needs to feel secure that adults in his life will not abandon him. His mother makes that point very clearly and is a source of strength and support. His special education teacher is gaining his respect by her continued support and belief in his ability to perform academically and make changes behaviorally. He believes the principal treats him fairly. All school staff should affirm Craig with their interactions, however brief. The counselor and school social worker will provide safe haven when it is needed. He has not been in a general education setting since fifth grade, and this is Craig's time, his school. He needs to belong. He has already met in a conflict resolution session with the youth he threatened, and both were satisfied with the outcome. Teaching staff will be alert to any signs of bullying by or directed at Craig and will manage this problem immediately with Life Space Crisis Intervention or referral, as appropriate. Adults in Craig's life will also encourage him to develop positive relationships with peers associated with his recreational interests.

Mastery: Although Craig has a history of underachieving, academics are his strongest area. He needs to be challenged intellectually and supported in his efforts to produce. He is proud of his achievements. Craig is self-conscious about his body image and often refuses to dress for gym. He should be encouraged to become involved in sports. This will put him in contact with a wider range of prosocial peers and provide opportunities to excel and create new images of himself as an athlete: a skier, a soccer team player.

Independence: After years of ineffective coping strategies, Craig needs to learn to take responsibility for himself and his actions. Craig will attend a weekly anger management group conducted by the court. In the past, Craig has not welcomed individual therapists who sought to reopen past issues such as possible abuse. Thus interventions will focus on practical and immediate "here and now" challenges Craig faces in school and relationships. Currently, Craig is subject to the routine consequences that apply to other students. Beyond this, problems arising in school will be viewed as errors in responding. In the event of any crises, these will be debriefed immediately by the counselor or principal, who will help Craig explore his thinking, feelings, and actions. The primary focus should be on cultivating his strengths and learning successful coping strategies. Because Craig is highly sensitive to criticism, staff will seek to be supportive and respectful as they help Craig learn to manage his emotions under stress, communicate without verbal hostility, and repair relationships with people with whom he has been in conflict. Craig is a very independent person, and the goal is to help him develop increased responsibility.

Generosity: Craig is beginning to think seriously about his future and purpose. Through his community service project of helping at the humane society, he is considering possible career options working with animals. He loves the animals. Craig is described as a warm, kindhearted person. He needs many opportunities to discover his own worth by reaching out to help others. Special education staff will arrange opportunities for Craig to tutor younger children. It is important that Craig cultivate caring and empathy. He wants to be liked and accepted and has great potential to contribute to others.

At the IEP conference, Craig was a full participant. During one part of the meeting, a section was devoted to listing his strengths. After staff read several of these items, he looked embarrassed and said with a shy smile, "OK, that's enough, let's get to the problems." Afterward, Craig felt good about this meeting and sought out his special education teacher for an extended positive discussion.

Those involved in Craig's life have no illusions that his problems are solved. The challenge will be to keep future setbacks from setting in motion a self-defeating cycle. As in the field of substance abuse, "relapses" should become opportunities to learn better strategies and get back on track. But for now, after years of fighting adults as hostile enemies, Craig has begun to travel a new pathway.

NOTES

[1] The Developmental Audit® is a registered trademark of the nonprofit organization Reclaiming Youth International, which provides training and certification in this assessment method. For information, contact Reclaiming Youth International, P.O. Box 57, Lennox, SD 57039.

[2] The first Developmental Audit was used in the case of a bullied 15-year-old youth, M. C., who shot three youths who came to his home to harass him. In the face of strong pressures to transfer the case to adult courts and prison, the presiding judge appointed Nicholas Long, from the Life Space Crisis Intervention Institute, and Larry Brendtro, from Reclaiming Youth, to develop an assessment and plan for intervention. On the basis of this report, the judge ruled that M. C. would receive treatment in the juvenile system. After two years in juvenile corrections, he was placed at Boys Town, Nebraska. While finishing high school, he worked as a computer technician for a group of psychologists. When M. C. graduated with honors, Father Val Peter of Boys Town reported that the youth thanked adults in his life "for giving me a name instead of a number." The young man completed a university degree in computer science and is now beginning his own family.

[3] These are examples of assessment and planning resources from a strength-based perspective: *The Behavioral and Emotional Rating Scale (BERS): A Strength-Based Approach to Assessment,* developed by Epstein and Sharma (1997), is published by PRO-ED, Austin,

Texas. *The Behavioral Objective Sequence (BOS)*, developed by Braaten (1998), is published by Research Press, Champaign, Illinois. Developmental Assets Inventories, developed by Peter Benson (1997) and colleagues, are available from Search Institute, Minneapolis, Minnesota.

[4] This process was developed in collaboration with staff from the Char-Em Intermediate School District, Charlevoix, Michigan.

[5] Larson and Van Paten (2000) developed two checklists of (a) psychosocial needs and (b) spiritual needs of youth, available on CD-ROM. The complete survey is appropriate for use by mentors in faith-based organizations. Here we draw from items on the psychosocial needs of children from the "What I Believe about Life" questionnaire. These items reflect research on resilience and alienation. Larson and Van Paten identify five dimensions: trust, competence, power, purpose, and self-sacrifice. We have combined the last two closely related concepts into "respect." This yields four dimensions that match the Circle of Courage resilience code.

[6] Most items are drawn from the needs assessment instrument of Larson and Van Paten (2000).

[7] Identifying information from the original document has been removed or altered.

CHAPTER 9

"The Courage to Trust"

ALLAN'S STORY

Allan is a 17-year-old youth whose life has been turbulent for as long as he can remember. He came to Allendale with a long history of family crises and less than effective interventions. His story of struggle is a powerful account of adversity and resilience.[1]

My adoption was arranged even before I was born. I went to a family who was loving but not very understanding. As long as I can remember, my parents fought. Just recently I got to look in my file, and I read in a report that my mom said Dad was "like the Gestapo." When Mom didn't cater to Dad, he would scream at her and hit her. One time right after she got an operation on her gall bladder, he kicked her in the stomach. When I watched them fight, I would be upset but I had a weird feeling of excitement. It must have really messed me up because, when I was 3, I would have nightmares and get up and go to the toilet in the corner of the room.

At age 5, I got kicked out of a preschool for continuously swearing and fighting. I liked first grade until I had to start writing. I loathe writing. I started slacking off because we had to write more and more, and I was having a hard time with that. My parents took me to doctors who gave me medication for ADHD. I didn't like reading out loud because my meds made me get some of the words wrong.

I know my dad meant well, but he didn't know how to properly love someone. He would punish me by putting soap in my mouth, and to get the taste out, he would go buy me a Dairy Queen. I wondered why was he taking me for ice cream right after he hit me. Probably so I would love him. Dad always wanted me to like him better than my mother. He tried to keep me all to himself. I was taught to hate my mom. Dad said she was a "bitch" and I should stay away from her. I was never allowed to spend much time with friends, either. It was psycho. He had a warped sense of love. Probably Dad needed to be in therapy more than me!

When I was 8, Dad started hitting me with a belt for my behaviors like arguing, talking back, or not doing my homework. I had to walk on pins and needles because the slightest thing might set him off. I was so much trouble for my parents that they started putting me in summer camps for problem kids. I had two dogs but lost both of them, one when I was sent to camp for being bad.

Shortly before I turned 13, I was removed from my family and placed in private boot camps in California and Idaho. Those places taught me how to destroy property and hide from people. They tried to control youth with levels and privileges. I never moved up because it required writing a page and a half about why I deserved the next level. It seemed hopeless, so I fought kids and I fought staff. They tried to force me to talk about my problems. These places were the first to require me to be in "group therapy." They all tried to get me to open up, and I had to try to block out nine people. Sometimes I slipped and they found out stuff about me. I tried to learn from that so I wouldn't let my guard down again. What is the point of letting people I don't trust know all about me?

After several months, I returned home. Being sent away did nothing to fix my problems with my family. Sometimes I hated Dad and wished him dead, but I never said it to anybody because Dad was also my best friend. Then when I was in seventh grade, he had a heart attack and died. Dad had taught me not to get along with my mom, and now I had to learn to live with her.

I was at school when Dad died. That morning when I said goodbye, I asked Dad if I could have five extra bucks cause it was pizza day. He said, "Yeah, sure, Allan." Then I said, "See you later. I love you." He said the same. Around lunchtime, I got a message that my dad's secretary was going to pick me up after school. He had already died but nobody told me.

Dad's secretary said we were going to the hospital, but she said, "Your dad had a heart attack but he is okay." I really wanted to see him and told her to hurry. When I walked into the hospital everyone was crying, and I said, "Why are you crying? Dad is okay, right?" They said, "No, Allan, your dad died." They said it happened around lunchtime. When I discovered I had been lied to, I had horrible feelings of anger.

My dad was doing something for me when he died. He was clipping branches off a tree so I could play basketball. My neighbor saw him fall down, tried to give him CPR, and called an ambulance. They said he had died within 10 seconds. Some people think I blame myself for his death but I don't. I knew he had a rare heart disease. My uncle, his twin brother, had died of the same thing. I had seen Dad with heart monitors and worried that he might die. But I told myself he wouldn't die at least until after I was done with college. When I think about it today, I realize we left on one of the better notes. But at the time I was totally stressed.

Dad died on Friday and I didn't have school for two days. On Monday, Mom said I didn't have to go to school if I didn't want to. But I said, "I want to, don't worry." I rode my bike to school on purpose, 'cause I didn't want to be at home, but I also didn't want to be at school. The folks at school said, "If you feel bad and want to go home, that is okay, we understand." So I said, "Oh, I am not feeling good. Can I please just leave?" I just wanted to escape. That day I rode my bike the farthest that I had ever ridden. I didn't come back home until about 8 at night.

I didn't go to the funeral home. I didn't want someone I barely even knew telling me, "I am so sorry he died." Why be sorry when someone dies? It's their time to go. I only cried maybe once. Now I just don't cry at all. I don't know why. I have never been much of a crier, just when I get physically hurt.

People think I should show feelings about what happened, that I am going to start crying about it or something. F—k it! I just turn my unhappiness into anger or sometimes into energy. I guess my brain purposely blocks the bad stuff that has happened to me. I put up a wall that is so strong, not even I can take it down. It will probably take a long time.

All through school I had problems fighting with other kids and teachers. But whenever I got in trouble, Dad would come to school, argue with school staff, and take my side. Now I was about to get in the worst trouble of my life, and he was not there to stand up for me.

I was in a special education class, and we had a substitute teacher I had never liked. She was like my dad, trying to dominate and control everything. On this particular day, we got into an argument about whether I would do a writing project on the computer or by hand. I don't mind working on the computer, but she wouldn't allow it. I got mad and told her, "You are wrong." She became angry and gave me an after-school detention. I told her, "I'm not serving your stupid detention," and called her a "bitch."

Then she said, "Oh, you will serve it all right. Your dad's not here to get you out of it this time!" I have never been so furious in my life. I looked her right in the eyes and told her, "I wish I could shoot you with a sawed-off shotgun!"

I was sent to the principal. The police were called. I ended up in a day school for behavior-disordered students. Some of the other kids and I started a fake gang, making fun of the school. We tipped over room dividers, dented desks, and did other mild vandalism. I purposely acted in ways to get disliked, and I refused to talk to counselors. Finally they decided to send me to a private residential treatment center in Maine.

I was ripped from my family and shipped halfway across the country. I hated this place and they hated me.

Kids who did something bad were sent to "The Corner" to sit all day. Then during the general meeting, the other kids were required to "confront" the person who had problems. They would surround you and yell, scream, and swear. If this didn't work, the group would restrain you on the floor. If the kids couldn't handle you, staff would use plastic ties on wrists and ankles. I hated being restrained and kept fighting them. When restraint wouldn't work, the next punishment was to place the kid in "The Ring." Staff put boxing gear on me. The other kids would surround me, joining arms. Three bigger, tougher boys took turns fighting me to teach me a lesson.

After a couple times in The Ring, I decided I had to do whatever it took to get out of that place. When restrained, I started spitting on people. Staff said, "Go ahead and spit, we are used to it." So, I came up with a better plan. I decided to do the grossest thing I could, which was to throw up on them, which really freaked them out. I am ashamed to talk about this and never did that since. But it got me out of that place, and if it came to that situation, I would do it again.

After leaving Maine, I returned to Illinois to enroll at Allendale. I didn't like being in another residential school, but I was able to be with my mother and sister on weekend visits. We began to become a family. I started succeeding in school. Before I was sent to Maine, I had stolen hundreds of dollars from my mother, so now I am working to get her trust. I have a good relationship with my sister, who teaches in Chicago; she was the only one I could turn to after Dad died.

At Allendale, I didn't get along with kids at first. I have been there for a year and have a lot of friends. I get along with most of the staff pretty well, too. What I like best is being able to work and earn money. I need to keep active or else I will go nuts. I hate being bored and want to be as adventuresome as I can in life. If I get stressed, I play sports or ride my bike or just read. Music isn't a very good escape for me because many of the popular songs are about death.

I am still careful about who I trust. People give off vibes, and I can tell whether they are safe or not. If I see someone I don't think I can trust, I will use any excuse to stay away from that person. If I am fooled at first, I back off later. After being forced to talk about my problems, I have trouble relating to counselors and therapists. It seems like they are trying to act like my friend just so they can find out shit about me. I usually say, "Leave me the hell alone." Most just give up.

Since I was a little kid, I have thought of being a veterinarian because animals are forgiving. Humans don't forgive or forget easily. When you get a bad reputation, some hold a grudge against you, like your name is Osama bin Laden. I sometimes wonder if people can forgive me.

Lately I have been thinking that if I don't become a vet, maybe I could be a psychologist. I would work with young kids before they really get messed up. I am just going to let them talk about whatever they want to talk about. If kids don't want to get close to you, don't try to force them and don't try to make them someone they don't want to be. Daring to trust is difficult, and I am the only one who knows when I am ready. That is why I decided to share my story. I only give this story to people who really care and have love in their heart.

NOTE

[1] Allan was a student at Allendale preparing to enroll in college when he shared this story.

A Life Space Crisis Intervention

"BUT I HAVE TO HAVE A BOYFRIEND!"

Bonnie McCarty (1998) shared this example of a Life Space Crisis Intervention she employed with Corrine, a junior high student who is so eager to keep her "boyfriend" that she allows him to put her down so that he can impress his peers. A teacher used this problem as an opportunity to help Corrine understand the true meaning of friendship.[1]

BACKGROUND OF THE PROBLEM

Corrine is a 12-year-old girl with a learning disability, attention problems, and impulsiveness. She has difficulty forming healthy peer friendships and becomes involved with students who degrade and tease her. Beyond school, her craving for friends has caused her to be misled into escapades she knows will get her into trouble. She feels bad about breaking rules but is unaware of how she is being taken advantage of and defends the actions of her "friends." Despite being active and noisy with peers, Corrine can be quiet and childlike around adults. When teased, she typically responds with a negative retort, digging herself into a worse situation.

The specific crisis incident began as Corrine stormed in from lunch just seconds before the tardy bell. I gave the class the usual directions to prepare for vocabulary practice. Corrine, obviously agitated, walked around the classroom, yelling put-downs at compliant peers. She found a seat at a table in the back, mumbling under her breath and refusing to work. I walked toward her and quietly stated that something seemed to be bothering her, and I gently, but firmly, reminded her that it is time for reading. Corrine pounded both hands on the table and yelled, "I can't take it anymore! Everybody is on me!" She went to the book corner, took a stuffed bear from the shelf, and sat on the floor, holding her knees and cradling the bear. I decide to employ Life Space Crisis Intervention strategies as described here.

Strategy 1: De-Escalate the Crisis Incident

I take a minute to reassure the other students in the class and to clarify the directions for their assigned independent vocabulary lesson. Then I move over to Corrine's corner.

Teacher: Corrine, as I look at you, it seems like you have a lot on your mind right now.

Corrine: He does it to me all the time. [Whining, puts head on knees.] Just leave me alone. I'm not going to talk to you.

Although Corrine's behavior is controlled, the baby talk, whining, and body language indicate she is still emotionally vulnerable. To foster discussion, I seek more privacy. An aide is available so I can have an opportunity to talk with Corrine:

Teacher: I understand that you want to be left alone, but perhaps it will be helpful if we talk about it.

Corrine: I don't want to talk. Nobody likes me. Just leave me alone.

Teacher: Corrine, I am impressed with how respectful you are being to the rest of the class, even though you are so upset. That shows a lot of maturity. Let's go into the hall, where we can have some privacy.

I stand up and move toward the door. Corrine quietly follows, head down. She carries the stuffed bear and mumbles under her breath. I thank Corrine for coming with me.

Strategy 2: Clarify the Timeline of What Happened

We move into the hall and sit next to each other in two class-room chairs. When I saw Corrine earlier in the day, things were going smoothly, so I suspected the triggering event might have happened during lunch. This would be my starting point. But before getting to the facts, I need to encourage Corrine to talk about the situation.

Teacher: Things were going all right this morning. That tells me something went wrong. Let's talk for a few min-utes so we can get to the bottom of this.

Corrine: I don't want to talk.

Teacher: I can understand not wanting to talk, but you are good at doing difficult tasks.

Corrine: *(Says nothing but plays with the stuffed bear in her lap.)*

Teacher: I am pleased you found that bear over by the book-shelf. He can be a good friend at times.

Corrine: I don't have any friends. I can't do anything right. Everyone makes everything my fault. He's always insulting me.

Teacher: What I saw earlier was a pretty happy young woman, and now I see you so upset. You feel you have no friends and get a lot of criticism.

Corrine begins talking rapidly, giving me a flood of information. Apparently there were problems at home over the weekend and her mother had called the school to discuss the problem with her guidance counselor, so Corrine was late getting to lunch.

Teacher: Wow! You do have a lot going on. Can you walk me back a step or two? What happened right before reading class?

Corrine: I didn't want to come to class but I did. I was real mad.

Teacher: So, even though you were mad, you came to class; I'm impressed! Help me understand what made you so mad.

Corrine: My dad is blaming it all on me, and it isn't true.

Teacher: What is your dad blaming you for?

Corrine: I've got too much pressure from my friends, and now I'm in so much trouble. I just want to call my mom and go home.

At this point I decide to back up and get a picture of the weekend's events in order to better understand how these events might have affected the current situation. Corrine talks freely, explaining that, on Sunday, Jeremy (her boyfriend) came over to visit. They were bored and looking for something else to do. Jeremy noticed a tie-dye project that Corrine's mother had begun and wanted to give it a try. Corrine initially resisted, but Jeremy called her stupid and chicken and threatened to leave because "you don't know how to have any fun." Despite the warnings of her parents not to make a mess, Corrine allowed Jeremy to talk her into tie-dyeing T-shirts in her room. The dye spilled all over the carpet, causing permanent damage. Jeremy hightailed it before Corrine's parents returned home, leaving her to face the problem alone. When Corrine's father discovered the stained carpet, he began criticizing Jeremy. Corrine got furious and yelled at her father, defending Jeremy. Her father then insisted the incident was Corrine's fault "because it is your room and you know the rules." (This is the Conflict Cycle in action.)

After Corrine relates the weekend disaster, she appears ready to begin focusing on "here and now" events in the cafeteria that led up to the explosion in reading class.

Teacher: Where did today's problem happen?

Corrine: At lunch.

Teacher: So what happened at lunch?

Corrine: Jeremy called me over to sit at the table where he was.

Teacher: Oh, so what did you think about that?

Corrine: I was pretty happy, except he was sitting with his friends and doesn't want anyone to know we are going out.

Teacher: So who else was sitting at the table with you?

Corrine: Jeremy's friends, Tony and Brad. I was the only girl.

Teacher: So what happened then?

Corrine: Tony started calling me names, making fun of me going to the counselor's office. He always insults me.

Teacher: How do you feel when that happens?

Corrine: I want to punch him out! Jeremy's friends don't like me. They want him all to themselves.

Teacher: What did Jeremy do after Tony started insulting you?

Corrine: He joined in like he always does.

Teacher: And how did that feel?

Corrine: But he's my boyfriend, so it's different.

Teacher: Wow! So you were getting it from all sides. You must have been feeling angry at this time, so what did you do?

Corrine: I told them to shut up and leave me alone!

Teacher: Did you say that softly?

Corrine: No way! I was steaming mad!

Teacher: Then what happened?

Corrine: Mr. Whelan came over and told me to go sit at the silence table until the bell rang. I wasn't even doing anything wrong!

Teacher: What thoughts were going through your head at the silence table?

Corrine: I was thinking about Tony and how he always does this to me. Jeremy doesn't want his friends to know we are going out. Now I'm not only in trouble at home, but at school, too.

Teacher: So your mind was full of thoughts and you were pretty upset. What happened when the bell rang?

Corrine: I left the lunchroom and went to my locker. Then I came to class.

Strategy 3: Diagnose the Meaning of the Behavior

After reviewing the timeline with Corrine and reflecting on the events of the weekend, it seems to me that the central issue is her willingness to be insulted and used by Jeremy so that he can have "fun" or look good to his peers. I decide to review the timeline in order to flesh out this self-defeating behavior pattern.

Teacher: Corrine, let me see if I understand what happened at lunch. You got to lunch late because the counselor needed to talk to you.

Corrine: Yeah, my mom had called her.

Teacher: So when Jeremy called you over to his table, you thought, 'Oh, good. I'll still get to sit with my boyfriend,' and felt relieved. Is this right so far?

Corrine: Yeah.

Teacher: Tony began teasing you about going to the counselor's office.

Corrine: Yeah, and that got me steamed; he's always starting trouble.

Teacher: So tell me again—what did Jeremy do?

Corrine: He started insulting me, too.

Teacher: He's your boyfriend, yet he was insulting you in front of his friends.

Corrine: Yeah.

Teacher: And how did you feel?

Corrine: Bad.

Teacher: So you were already feeling bad, and your boyfriend, a person who is supposed to think you're special, adds fuel to the fire.

Corrine: But he was just teasing.

Teacher: Does he do this often?

Corrine: Yeah.

Teacher: It sounds a lot like what happened this weekend. Do you feel happy when you're with Jeremy?

Corrine: I don't know.

Teacher: Is it better for you to be with Jeremy?

Corrine: Yeah, because I feel dumb if I don't have a boyfriend.

Strategy 4: Promote Insight and Accountability

Although Corrine is intent on differentiating Jeremy's teasing and insults from that of his friends, I decide to attempt to help her realize how Jeremy's actions toward her are not compatible with those of a caring friend, and that in fact she is being exploited.

Teacher: I hear you say that today you came to school feeling bad about your weekend with Jeremy. You had a good morning, but then the counselor talked to you and you went to lunch worried and a little mad. Today, like lots of days, Jeremy joined in the teasing, and you felt angry and ended up at the silent table. Then you came to reading and exploded in class. So what happens to Corrine?

Corrine: I don't get my work done.

Teacher: Right. So does life get better or worse for you?

Corrine: Worse.

Teacher: Corrine, I have a thought. Do you think that someone who cares about you would want you to get into trouble?

Corrine: No, not on purpose.

Teacher: Then help me understand this. Jeremy's your boyfriend—right?

Corrine: Yeah.

Teacher: But he doesn't want you to tell anyone.

Corrine: Right.

Teacher: He doesn't want you to tell anyone, but he comes over to your house, like on Sunday, and even though you told him the rules, he talked you into tie-dyeing.

Corrine: Right. He said I was stupid to be worried.

Teacher: Right. He called you names and insulted you. And then today at lunch you were feeling bad, Tony was teasing you, and Jeremy joined in.

Corrine: Yes, he's always insulting me and treating me bad in front of people, and I get in trouble.

Teacher: Corrine, say that again. *(I ask her to repeat this comment to highlight her fledgling insight, and she obliges.)* That's right, Corrine. He teases you so he can have fun and look good to his friends. You get mad or get caught and pay the price.

Corrine: He should help pay for the rug.

Teacher: You're absolutely right—a true friend would share that responsibility. So is it fair to say that Jeremy likes to break the rules and insult you, and even though you know the rules and it makes you feel bad, you go along in order to keep him as your boyfriend?

Corrine: Yes, because you have to have a boyfriend.

Teacher: So does your life get better or worse when you go along with Jeremy?

Corrine: I don't know.

Teacher: Do you feel happy when you're with Jeremy?

Corrine: I don't know.

Teacher: Is it better for you?

Corrine: Yeah, because I have a boyfriend.

Teacher: And that's important to you?

Corrine: Yeah, I feel dumb if I don't have a boyfriend.

Teacher: So in order not to feel dumb, you hang with Jeremy, but you said Jeremy makes you feel bad.

Corrine: Only sometimes. I thought he might be abusing me as a friend.

Teacher: Say that again. *(I am seeking to make this idea more prominent in her thinking.)*

If you're feeling bad, and he makes you feel worse, is that being a good friend?

Corrine: No.

Teacher: Have you ever thought that perhaps Jeremy is not the right boyfriend for you?

Corrine: I think about it. But it will be hard because he'll insult me more if I break up with him.

Corrine has stated the problem and is probably not ready to push the insight further. Whenever I discussed breaking up with Jeremy, she resorted to defensive "I don't know" answers and justified keeping the relationship intact. Her private logic can be summarized thus: "If I dump Jeremy, he'll still insult me and no other boys will like me. I have to have a boyfriend to get a better one." Still, seeds have been planted, and Corrine has new ways of thinking about this problem relationship. It is time to turn to more short-term goals. I praise Corrine and support her realization that she needs to find a way to remove herself from Jeremy's negative influence.

Strategy 5: Teach Prosocial Coping Skills

I focus back on the lunchroom incident in order to give Corrine skills to break this pattern of exploitation and abuse. Together we look at how to handle Jeremy and his friends in the future. I begin by saying, "It sounds like we need a plan to handle this insulting-at-lunch problem." Although Corrine is not ready to totally sever this relationship with Jeremy, she is eager to develop strategies to disengage her from trouble if it happens again. She comes up with several options, including the following:

- Don't sit with him if he's with his friends.
- Ignore him when he teases.
- Move to another table if the teasing starts.

Because the lunchroom is the staging ground for this problem, we decide to enlist the help of Mr. Whelan, the lunchroom supervisor, so he might be able to provide some support if something like this happens again. We sort through the concrete steps to make the plan happen and decide to begin by setting up an appointment with Mr. Whelan. We discuss how Mr. Whelan might feel about talking today because Corrine had been in trouble in the lunchroom. We practice how Corrine could control her tone of voice and body language if faced with a gruff attitude from Mr. Whelan. After talking about our plan, we role-play making an appointment, and Corrine is smiling and confident when we finish.

Strategy 6: Transfer Learning to the Life Space

This one intervention will not cause lasting change because Corrine still does not yet have the confidence to leave Jeremy. Still, in the short term, she can learn to be more assertive in disengaging from abuse. Her teacher, counselor, and other adults can support her in gaining enough confidence to choose friends who won't hurt her. Corrine is in a good mood and is ready to return to class. I review her assignment and remind her that she can complete it after the class project that is about to begin. We enter class together, and I transition the class from independent work to the group lesson.

This example of LSCI began with a specific incident that involved inappropriate classroom behavior. It could have been handled by exclusion, but the opportunity to understand Corrine and give her more effective coping strategies would have been sacrificed. We see that Corrine's self-worth is tied to her need to be viewed as having a boyfriend, however badly he treats her. She came to the point of sharing that she has thought of breaking away from Jeremy but fears he might then humiliate her even more. If Corrine were to continue on this pathway of allowing others to mistreat her, in a few years one might see a classic case of an abused wife. This issue is now on her mind, and future problems can begin where this "lesson" ended. Corrine is rethinking her choices in setting the pathway of her life.

NOTE

[1] Adapted from McCarty (1998) with permission of the journal *Reclaiming Children and Youth*.

References

Aber, J., Brown, J., & Henrich, C. (1999). *Teaching conflict resolution: An effective school-based approach to violence prevention.* Research brief. New York: National Center for Children in Poverty, Columbia University.

Achenbach, T. M. (2000). Assessment of psychopathology. In A. J. Sameroff, M. Lewis, & S. M. Miller (Eds.), *Handbook of developmental psychopathology* (2nd ed., pp. 41–56). New York: Plenum.

Addams, J. (1909). *The spirit of youth and the city streets.* New York: Macmillan.

Aggleton, J. P. (Ed.). (2000). *The amygdala: A functional analysis* (2nd ed.). Oxford, UK: Oxford University Press.

Aichhorn, A. (1935). *Wayward youth.* New York: Viking.

Ainsworth, M. D. S. (1989). Attachments beyond infancy. *American Psychologist, 44*, 709–716.

Alexander, F., & Selesnick, S. (1966). *The history of psychiatry: An evaluation of psychiatric thought and practice from prehistoric times to the present.* New York: Harper & Row.

Allport, G. (1937). *Personality: A psychological interpretation.* New York: Henry Holt.

American Academy of Child and Adolescent Psychiatry [AACAP]. (2002). Practice parameter for the prevention and management of aggressive behavior in child and adolescent psychiatric institutions, with special reference to seclusion and restraint. *Child and Adolescent Psychiatry, 41* (Suppl.) 4S-25S.

American Psychiatric Association. (2000). *Diagnostic and statistical manual of mental disorders* (4th ed. text revision). Washington, DC: Author.

Anastopoulos, A., & Shaffer, S. (2001). Attention deficit/hyperactivity disorder. In C. E. Walker & M. C. Roberts (Eds.), *Handbook of clinical child psychology* (pp. 470–494). New York: Wiley.

Angyal, A. (1965). *Neurosis & treatment: A holistic theory.* New York: Wiley.

Anthony, E .J., & Cohler, B. J. (Eds.). (1987). *The invulnerable child.* New York: Guilford.

Araji, S. K. (1997). *Sexually aggressive children: Can we understand them?* Thousand Oaks, CA: Sage.

Artz, S., Nicholson, D., Halsall, E., & Larke, S. (2001). *Guide for needs assessment for youth.* Victoria, BC: University of Victoria.

Augustine. (1923). *The confessions of St. Augustine.* (T. Matthew, Trans.) London: Collins.

Babel, D. J. (1993). Parenting a raging child. *Journal of Emotional and Behavioral Problems, 2*(1), 7.

Baker, S., & Gersten, R. (2000, July 14). *Balancing qualitative/quantitative research.* Paper presented at OSEP Research Project Director's Conference, Washington, DC.

Bandura, A. (1977). Self-efficacy: Toward a unifying theory of behavior change. *Psychological Review, 84,* 191–215.

Bandura, A. (Ed.). (1995). *Self-efficacy in changing societies.* Cambridge, UK: Cambridge University Press.

Barber, B. K., Bean, R. L., & Erickson, L. D. (2002). Expanding the study and understanding of psychological control. In B. K. Barber (Ed.), *Intrusive parenting: How psychological control affects children and adolescents* (pp. 263–289). Washington, DC: American Psychological Association.

Barber, B. K., & Harmon, E. L. (2002). Violating the self: Parental psychological control of children and adolescents. In B. K. Barber (Ed.), *Intrusive parenting: How psychological control affects children and adolescents* (pp. 15–52). Washington, DC: American Psychological Association.

Beck, A. (1999). *Prisoners of hate: The cognitive basis of anger, hostility, and violence.* New York: HarperCollins.

Bell-Dolan, D., & Anderson, C. A. (1999). Attributional processes: An integration of social and clinical psychology. In R. Kowalski & M. R. Leary (Eds.), *The social psychology of emotional and behavioral problems: Interfaces of social and clinical psychology* (pp. 37–68). Washington, DC: American Psychological Association.

Benson, P. L. (1997). *All kids are our kids: What communities must do to raise caring and responsible children and adolescents.* San Francisco: Jossey-Bass.

Berg, I. K. (1994). *Family based services.* New York: W. W. Norton.

Bettelheim, B. (1967). *The empty fortress.* New York: Free Press.

Bockhoven, J. S. (1956). Moral treatment in American psychiatry. *The Journal of Nervous and Mental Disease, 124*(2, 3), 167–194, 292–321.

Bower, E. (1969). *Early identification of emotionally handicapped children in school* (2nd ed.). Springfield, IL: Charles C Thomas.

Bowlby, J. (1982). *Attachment and loss (Vol. 1).* New York: Basic Books.

Braaten, S. (1988). *The Behavioral Objective Sequence (BOS).* Champaign, IL: Research Press.

Bradley, E. L., & Bradley, M. Menefee. (1926). *Allendale annals.* Lake Villa, IL: Annandale Press.

Bradley, S. J. (2000). Affect regulation and the development of psychopathology. New York: Guilford.

Braune, J. (2001). Children in the American Gulag. *Reclaiming Children and Youth, 10*(2), 81–82.

Brendtro, L., & Bacon, J. (1995). Youth empowerment and teamwork. In H. Garner (Ed.), *Teamwork models and experience in education and child care* (pp. 55–71). New York: Prentice Hall.

Brendtro, L., & Banbury, J. (1994). Tapping the strengths of oppositional youth: Helping Kevin change. *Journal of Emotional and Behavioral Problems, 3*(2), 41–45.

Brendtro, L., Brokenleg, M., & Van Bockern, S. (1990, 2002). *Reclaiming youth at risk: Our hope for the future.* Bloomington, IN: National Educational Service.

Brendtro, L., & Cunningham, J. (1999). Meeting developmental needs of incarcerated youth. *Reclaiming Children and Youth, 7*(2), 104–109.

Brendtro, L., & Hinders, D. (1990). A saga of Janusz Korczak, the king of children. *Harvard Educational Review, 60*(2), 237–246.

Brendtro, L., & Ness, A. (1982). Perspectives on peer group treatment: The use and abuse of Guided Group Interaction/Positive Peer Culture. *Children and Youth Services Review, 4,* 307–324.

Brendtro, L., Ness, A., & Mitchell, M. (2001). *No disposable kids.* Longmont, CO: Sopris West.

Bronfenbrenner, U. (1986). Alienation and the four worlds of childhood. *Phi Delta Kappan, 67,* 430–436.

Brown, B. B. (1990). Peer groups and peer cultures. In S. S. Feldman & G. R. Eliot (Eds.), *At the threshold* (pp. 171–196). Cambridge, MA: Harvard University Press.

Brown, W. (1983). *The other side of delinquency.* New Brunswick, NJ: Rutgers University Press.

Bruner, J. (1990). *Acts of meaning.* Cambridge, MA: Harvard University Press.

Buehler, R. E., Patterson, G. R., & Furniss, J. M. (1966). The reinforcement of behavior in institutional settings. *Behaviour Research and Therapy, 4,* 157–167.

Buetler, L., & Malik, M. (Eds.). (2002). *Rethinking DSM: A psychological perspective.* Washington, DC: American Psychological Association.

Cairns, R. B., & Cairns, B. D. (1994.) *Lifelines and risks: Pathways of youth in our times.* New York: Cambridge University Press.

Cairns, R. B., & Cairns, B. D. (2000). The natural history and developmental functions of aggression. In A. J. Sameroff, M. Lewis, & S. Miller (Eds.), *Handbook of developmental psychopathology* (2nd ed., pp. 403–429). New York: Plenum.

Caplan, G. (1964). *Principles of preventive psychiatry.* New York: Basic Books.

Caspy, A., & Moffitt, T. (1995). The continuity of maladaptive behavior: From description to understanding in the study of antisocial behavior. In D. Cicchetti & D. J. Cohen (Eds.), *Developmental psychopathology: Vol. 2. Risk disorder and adaptation* (pp. 472–511). New York: Wiley.

Cassidy, J. (1999). The nature of the child's ties. In J. Cassidy & P. R. Shaver (Eds.), *Handbook of attachment* (pp. 3–20). New York: Guilford.

Center, D. B., & Calloway, J. M. (1999). Self-reported job stress and personality in teachers of students with emotional or behavioral disorders. *Behavioral Disorders, 25*(1), 41–51.

Chamberlain, P., Fisher, P., & Moore, K. (2002). Multidimensional treatment foster care: Applications of the OSLC intervention model to high-risk youth and their families. In J. Reid, G. R. Patterson,

& J. Snyder (Eds.), *Antisocial behavior in children and adolescents.* Washington, DC: American Psychological Association.

Chambers, J. C. (2000). Unmasking the terror. *Reclaiming Children and Youth, 9*(1), 14–16.

Chess, S., & Thomas, A. (1986). *Temperament in clinical practice.* New York: Guilford.

Children's Defense Fund. (2001). *Children's Defense Fund 2001 Yearbook.* Washington, DC: Author.

Cicchetti, D., & Lynch, M. (1995). Failures in the respectable environment and their impact on individual development: The case of child maltreatment. In D. Cicchetti & D. J. Cohen (Eds.), *Developmental psychopathology: Vol. 2. Risk disorder and adaptation* (pp. 32–71). New York: Wiley.

Clark, M. (2001). Influencing positive behavior change: Increasing the therapeutic approach of juvenile courts. *Federal Probation, 65*(1), 8–28.

Cline, M. (1997, April 23). Looking at both sides of the issue. *The Cherokee Tribune* [Waleska, Georgia], p. 4A.

Cohn, J. (1996). *Raising compassionate, courageous children in a violent world.* Atlanta: Longstreet.

Coles, R. (1990). *The spiritual life of children.* Boston: Houghton Mifflin.

Coopersmith, S. (1967). *The antecedents of self esteem.* San Francisco: Freeman.

Crisis Prevention Institute. (2002). Training yields positive results. *Reclaiming Children and Youth, 10*(4), 251–252.

Csikszentmihalyi, M. (1990). *Flow: The psychology of optimal experience.* New York: HarperCollins.

Csikszentmihalyi, M. (1996). *Creativity: Flow and the psychology of discovery and invention.* New York: HarperCollins.

Curwin, R., & Mendler, A. (1999). *Discipline for dignity with challenging youth.* Bloomington, IN: National Educational Service.

Darwin, C. (1998). *The expression of emotions in man and animals* (3rd ed.). New York: Oxford University Press. (Original work published 1872)

Davis, H. H. (1928). Corporal punishment and suspension. *School and Society, 28,* 630.

Dawson, C. A. (2001). *Crisis intervention training and support for school staff of junior high school special education students with emotional disturbances.* Doctoral dissertation. Nova Southeastern University.

Dawson, C. A. (2003). A study on the effectiveness of Life Space Crisis Intervention for students identified with emotional disturbance. *Reclaiming Children and Youth, 11*(4), 223–230.

de Becker, G. (1998). *The gift of fear.* New York: Dell.

Deloria, E. C. (1943). *Speaking of Indians.* New York: Friendship Press.

de Mause, L. (Ed.). (1974). *The history of childhood.* Northvale, NJ: Aaronson.

Derryberry, D., & Rothbart, M. K. (1997). Reactive and effortful processes in the organization temperament. *Development and Psychopathology, 9,* 633–652.

Dewey, J. (1913). *Interest and effort in education.* Carbondale, IL: Southern Illinois University Press.

Dewey, J. (1933). *How we think.* Boston: D. C. Heath.

Diel, P. (1987). *The psychology of reeducation.* (Raymond Rosenthal, Trans.). Boston: Chambhala.

Dishion, T., French, D., & Patterson, G. R. (1995). The development and ecology of antisocial behavior. In D. Cicchetti & D. J. Cohen (Eds.), *Developmental psychopathology: Vol. 2. Risk disorder and adaptation* (pp. 421–471). New York: Wiley.

Dishion, T., McCord, J., & Poulin, F. (1999). When interventions harm: Peer groups and problem behavior. *American Psychologist, 54*(9), 755–764.

Dix, D. (1845). *Prisons and prison discipline in the United States.* Philadelphia: Joseph Kite.

Docking, J. (Ed.). (1990). *Education and alienation in the junior school.* London: Falmer.

Dodge, K. A. (1993). Social-cognitive mechanisms in the development of conduct disorder and depression. *Annual Review of Psychology, 44,* 559–584.

Donovan, J., Jesser, R., & Costa, S. (1988). Syndrome of problem behavior in adolescents: A replication. *Journal of Consulting and Clinical Psychology, 56,* 762–765.

Doucette, A. (2002). Child and adolescent diagnosis: The need for a model-based approach. In L. Buetler & M. Malik (Eds.),

Rethinking DSM: A psychological perspective (pp. 201–220). Washington, DC: American Psychological Association.

Dubner, A., & Motta, R. (1999). Sexually and physically abused foster care children and posttraumatic stress disorder. *Journal of Consulting and Clinical Psychology, 67*(3), 367–373.

Ducharme, J., Atkinson, L., & Poulton, L. (2000). Success based, non-coercive treatment of oppositional behavior in children from violent homes. *Journal of Child and Adolescent Psychiatry, 39*(8), 995–1007.

Duchnowski, A. J., & Kutash, K. (1996). The mental health perspective. In C. M. Nelson, R. B. Rutherford, & B. I. Wolford (Eds.), *Comprehensive and collaborative systems that work for troubled youth: A national agenda* (pp. 90–110). Richmond, KY: National Coalition for Juvenile Justice Services.

Duncan, B. L., Hubble, M. A., & Miller, S. D. (1997). *Psychotherapy with "impossible" cases: The efficient treatment of therapy veterans*. New York: Norton.

du Toit, L. (1997). *Developmental assessment for children, youth, and families*. Pretoria, South Africa: Interministerial Committee for Young Persons at Risk.

Eber, L., Nelson, C. Michael, & Miles, P. (1997). School-based wraparound for students with emotional and behavioral challenges. *Exceptional Children, 63*(4), 539–555.

Echo Bridge Productions (1996). *The legacy of childhood trauma: Not always who they seem*. Champaign, IL: Research Press. [Discussion guide to a video series with the same title]

Edelstien, G. M. (1990). *Symptom analysis: Method of brief therapy*. New York: Norton.

Eisenberg, L. (2001). The past fifty years of child and adolescent psychiatry: A personal memoir. *Child and Adolescent Psychiatry, 40*(7), 743–747.

Emery, R. E., & Kitzmann, K. M. (1995). The child in the family: Disruptions in family functions. In D. Cicchetti & D. J. Cohen (Eds.), *Developmental psychopathology: Vol. 2. Risk disorder and adaptation* (pp. 3–31). New York: Wiley.

Epstein, M. H., Kutash, K., & Duchnowski, A. (Eds.). (1998). *Outcomes for children and youth with behavioral and emotional disorders and their families: Programs and evaluation best practices*. Austin, TX: PRO-ED.

Epstein, M. H., & Sharma, J. (1997). *Behavioral and emotional rating scale: A strength-based approach to assessment.* Austin, TX: PRO-ED.

Epstein S., and Meier, P. (1989). Constructive thinking: A broad coping variable with specific components. *Journal of Personality and Social Psychology, 57,* 332–350.

Erikson, E. (1963). *Childhood and society.* New York: W. W. Norton.

Eysenck, H. J. (1970). *The structure of human personality* (3rd ed.). London: Methuen.

Eysenck, H. J. (1997). Personality and the biosocial model of anti-social criminal behavior. In A. Raine, P. Brennan, D. Farrington, & S. Mednick (Eds.), *Biosocial bases of violence* (pp. 21–37). New York: Plenum.

Fahlberg, V. I. (1991). *A child's journey through placement.* Indianapolis, IN: Perspectives.

Farmer, T., & Hollowell, J. (1994). Social networks in mainstream classrooms: Social affiliations and behavior characteristics of students with EBD. *Journal of Emotional and Behavioral Disorders, 2*(2), 143–155.

Feldman, R. A. (1992). The St. Louis experiment: Effective treatment of anti-social youths in prosocial groups. In J. McCord & R. A. Tremblay (Eds.), *Preventing anti-social behavior: Interventions from birth through adolescence* (pp. 233–252). New York: Guilford.

Fine, M. (1991). *Framing dropouts: Notes on the politics of an urban public high school.* Albany: State University of New York Press.

Finkelhor, D., & Browne, A. (1985, October). The traumatic impact of child-sexual abuse: A conceptualization. *American Journal of Orthopsychiatry, 55*(4), 530–541.

Finkelhor, D., & Williams, L. Meyer. (1990, April 25). *Male sexuality and the sexualization of emotions: Developing a scale to predict child molesting.* Report on a research grant from the National Center on Child Abuse and Neglect (CA-90-1377) and the Northstar Foundation.

Forness, S. R., Kavale, K. A., & Crenshaw, T. M. (1999). Stimulant medication revisited: Effective treatment of children with ADHD. *Reclaiming Children and Youth, 7*(4), 230–233.

Frankl, V. (1984). *Man's search for meaning.* New York: Touchstone Books.

Friesen, B. J., & Stephens, B. (1998). Expanding family roles in the system of care: Research and practice. In M. H. Epstein, K. Kutash, & A. Duchnowski (Eds.), *Outcomes for children and youth with behavioral and emotional disorders and their families: Programs and evaluation best practices* (pp. 231–260). Austin, TX: PRO-ED.

Fromm, E. (1998). Lost and found half a century later: Letters by Freud and Einstein. *American Psychologist 53*(10), 1195–1198.

Fulcher, L. C. (2001). Cultural safety: Lessons from Maori wisdom. *Reclaiming Children and Youth, 10*(3), 153–157.

Furstenberg, F., Jr., Cook, T., Eccles, J., Elder, G., Jr., & Sameroff, A. (1999). *Managing to make it: Urban families and adolescent success*. Chicago: University of Chicago.

Gable, R. A., Quinn, M. M., Rutherford, R. B., Jr., Howell, K. W., & Hoffman, C. C. (1998). *Addressing student problem behavior: Part II. An IEP team's introduction to functional behavioral assessment and behavior intervention plans*. Washington, DC: Center for Effective Collaboration and Practice.

Gable, R. A., Quinn, M. M., Rutherford, R. R., Howell, K. W., & Hoffman, C. C. (2000). *Creating positive behavioral intervention plans and supports* (2nd ed.). Washington, DC: Center for Effective Collaboration, American Institutes for Research.

Gabor, P., & Greene, I. (1991). Views from the inside: Young people's perceptions of residential services. *Journal of Child and Youth Care Work, 7,* 6–19.

Gallagher, M. (2000). The amygdala and associative learning. In J. P. Aggleton (Ed.), *The amygdala: A functional analysis* (2nd ed., pp. 311–329). Oxford, UK: Oxford University Press.

Garbarino, J., & Eckenrode, J. (1997). *Understanding abusive families: An ecological approach to theory and practice*. San Francisco: Jossey-Bass.

Giacobbe, G., Traynelis-Yurek, E., & Laursen, E. (1999). *Strength based strategies for children & youth: An annotated bibliography*. Richmond, VA: G & P.

Gibbs, J. (1994). Fairness and empathy as the foundation for universal moral education. *Comenius, 14,* 12–23.

Gibbs, J., Potter, G., & Goldstein, A. P. (1995). *The EQUIP program: Teaching youth to think and act responsibly through a peer-helping approach*. Champaign, IL: Research Press.

Gibbs, J., Potter, G., Goldstein, A. P., & Brendtro, L. (1996). From harassment to helping with anti-social youth: The EQUIP program. *Reclaiming Children and Youth, 5*(1), 40–46.

Gibbs, J., Potter, G., Goldstein, A. P., & Brendtro, L. (1998). How EQUIP programs help youth change. *Reclaiming Children and Youth, 7*(2),117–172.

Gilligan, C., Rogers, A., & Tolman, D. (Eds.). (1991). *Women, girls, and psychotherapy: Reframing resistance.* New York: Haworth.

Glantz, K., & Pearce, J. K. (1989). *Exiles from Eden: Psychotherapy from an evolutionary perspective.* New York: Norton.

Gold, M. (1974). A time for skepticism. *Crime and Delinquency, 20,* 20–24.

Gold, M. (1978). Scholastic experiences, self-esteem, and delinquent behavior: A theory for alternative schools. *Crime and Delinquency, 24*(3), 290–308.

Gold, M. (1995). Charting a course: Promise and prospects for alternative schools. *Journal of Emotional and Behavioral Problems, 3*(4), 8–11.

Gold, M., & Mann, D. W. (1984). *Expelled to friendlier places.* Ann Arbor: University of Michigan Press.

Gold, M., & Osgood, D. W. (1992). *Personality and peer influence in juvenile correction.* Westport, CT: Greenwood.

Goldstein, A. P. (1993). Interpersonal skills training intervention. In A. P. Goldstein and C. R. Huff (Eds.), *The gang intervention handbook* (pp. 87–157). Champaign, IL: Research Press.

Goldstein, A. P. (1999). *The Prepare Curriculum: Teaching prosocial competencies* (Rev. ed.). Champaign, IL: Research Press.

Goldstein, A. P. (2001). *Reducing resistance: Methods for enhancing openness to change.* Champaign, IL: Research Press.

Goldstein, A. P., & Glick, B. (1994). *The prosocial gang: Implementing aggression replacement training.* Thousand Oaks, CA: Sage.

Goldstein, A. P., & Martens, B. K. (2000). *Lasting change: Methods for enhancing generalization of gain.* Champaign, IL: Research Press.

Goldstein, A. P., & McGinnis, E. (1997). *Skillstreaming the adolescent* (Rev. ed.). Champaign, IL: Research Press.

Goleman, D. (1995). *Emotional intelligence.* New York: Bantam Books.

Graham, M. T. (1985, December). *The concept of structure in residential treatment programs.* Master's thesis, Arizona State University.

Greenberg, M. T., Bierman, K., Cole, J. D., Dodge, K. A., Lochman, J. E., & McMahon, J. (1998, August). *Results of the FASTTrack Prevention Trial.* Presentation to the American Psychological Association, San Francisco.

Hallowell, E. M. (1999). *Connect.* New York: Simon & Schuster.

Halstrom, L. (Director), & Gladstein, R. N. (Producer). (1999). *Cider house rules* [Motion picture]. United States: Miramax Films.

Hanna, F. J. (2002). *Therapy with difficult clients.* Washington, DC: American Psychological Association.

Harris, J. R. (1998). *The nurture assumption: Why children turn out the way they do.* New York: Free Press.

Hauser, S., & Bowlds, M. K. (1990). Stress, coping, and adaptation. In S. S. Feldman & G. R. Elliot (Eds.), *At the threshold: The developing adolescent.* Cambridge, MA: Harvard University Press.

Heider, F. (1958). *The psychology of interpersonal relations.* New York: Wiley.

Henggeler, S., Schenwald, S., Borduin, C., Rowland, M., & Cunningham, P. (1998). *Multisystemic treatment of antisocial behavior in children and adolescents.* New York: Guilford.

Hibbler, W. J., & Shahbazian, M. (1999). We cannot afford to fail them: A dialogue with the presiding judge of the world's first juvenile court. *Reclaiming Children and Youth, 8*(3), 145–150.

Hill, P. (1993). Recent advances of selected aspects of adolescent development. *Journal of Child Psychology and Psychiatry, 34,* 69–99.

Hobbs, N. (1994). *The troubled and troubling child.* Cleveland: AREA.

Hoffman, M. L. (2002). Toward a comprehensive empathy-based theory of pro-social development. In A. Bohart & D. Stipek (Eds.), *Constructive & destructive behavior: Implications for family, school, and society* (pp. 61–86). Washington, DC: American Psychological Association.

Hoover, J., & Milner, C. (1998). Are hazing and bullying related to love and belongingness? *Reclaiming Children and Youth, 7*(3), 138–141.

Hubble, M., Duncan, B., & Miller, S. (1999). *The heart and soul of change*. Washington, DC: American Psychological Association.

Huff, B. (2001, Summer). Providing a national voice for families of children with mental health needs. *Claiming Children*. (Publication of the Federation of Families for Children's Mental Health, 1021 Prince Street, Alexandria, VA 22314-2971)

Hughes, J. (Director). (1985). *The breakfast club* [Motion picture]. United States: Universal Studios.

Hyman, I., & Snook, P. (2001). Dangerous schools, alienated students. *Reclaiming Children and Youth, 10*(3), 133–136.

Irving, J. (1985). *Cider house rules*. New York: William & Morrow.

Isen, A. M. (2000). Positive affect and decision-making. In M. Lewis & J. M. Haviland-Jones (Eds.), *Handbook of emotions* (2nd ed., pp. 417–435). New York: Guilford.

Izard, C. E., & Ackerman, B. P. (2000). Motivational, organizational, and regulatory functions of discrete emotions. In M. Lewis & J. M. Haviland-Jones (Eds.), *Handbook of emotions* (2nd ed., pp. 253–264). New York: Guilford.

Joint Commission on Accreditation of Health Care Organizations [JCAHCO]. (2001). *2001–2002 comprehensive accreditation manual for behavioral health care*. Oakbrook Terrace, IL: Author.

Kauffman, J. M. (2000). Future directions with troubled children. *Reclaiming Children and Youth, 9*(2), 119–124.

Kelley, B. Tatem, Thornberry, T. P., & Smith, C. A. (1997, August). In the wake of childhood maltreatment. *Juvenile Justice Bulletin*. (OJJDP)

Kemp, S. P., Whittaker, J. K., & Tracy, E. M. (1997). *Person-environment practice: The social ecology of interpersonal helping*. New York: Aldine de Gruyter.

Kessler, R. (2000). *The soul of education: Helping students find connection, compassion and character at school*. Alexandria, VA: ASCD.

Kevin [pseudonym]. (1994). My independence day. *Journal of Emotional and Behavioral Problems, 3*(2), 35–40.

Key, E. (1909). *The century of the child*. New York: Putnam.

Kipnis, A. (1999). *Angry young men: How parents, teachers, and counselors can help bad boys become good men*. San Francisco: Jossey-Bass.

Knitzer, J., Steinberg, Z., & Fleisch, B. (1990). *At the schoolhouse door*. New York: Bank Street College of Education.

Kress, C., & Randall, H. K. (Eds.). (1998). *BOOMERANG! Character education program*. Prepared by B. Ranum, C. Baumgartner, & V. Grover. Ames: Iowa State University Extension, 4-H Youth Development.

Kusché, C. A., & Greenberg, M. T. (in press). Brain development and social-emotional learning: An introduction for educators. In M. Elias, H. Arnold, & C. Steiger (Eds.), *Fostering knowledgeable, responsible and caring students*. New York: Teachers College Press.

Lantieri, L. (2001). *Schools with spirit: Nurturing the inner lives of children and teachers*. Boston: Beacon.

Lantieri, L., & Patti, J. (1996). *Waging peace in our schools*. Boston: Beacon.

Larson, R. (2000). Toward a psychology of positive youth development. *American Psychologist, 55*(1), 170–183.

Larson, S., & Brendtro, L. (2000). *Reclaiming our prodigal sons and daughters*. Bloomington, IN: National Educational Service.

Larson, S., & Van Paten, D. (2000). *Quick Connect: CD-ROM tool to discover individual spiritual needs of youth*. Loveland, CO: Group Publishing.

Laursen, E. K. (2000). Strength-based practice with children in trouble. *Reclaiming Children and Youth, 9*(2), 70–75.

Lazarus, R. S., & Folkman, S. (1984). *Stress, appraisal, and coping*. New York: Springer.

LeDoux, J. (1996). *The emotional brain*. New York: Simon & Schuster.

LeDoux, J., & Phelps, E. (2000). Emotional networks in the brain. In M. Lewis & J. M. Haviland-Jones (Eds.), *Handbook of emotions* (2nd ed., pp. 157–172). New York: Guilford.

Levy, F., Hay, D., McStephen, M., Wood, C., & Waldman, I. (1997, June). Attention-deficit hyperactivity disorder: A category or a continuum? Genetic analysis of a large-scale twin study. *Journal of the American Academy of Child & Adolescent Psychiatry, 36*(6), 737–744.

Lewis, M. (2000). Toward a development of psychopathology. In A. J. Sameroff, M. Lewis, & S. Miller (Eds.), *Handbook of developmental psychology* (2nd ed., pp. 3–22). New York: Plenum.

Lewis, R. G. (2002, April 26). Adolescents and families for life. Presentation to the annual conference of the United Methodist Association of Health and Welfare Ministries, Charlotte, NC.

Lickona, T. (2001). What is good character? And how can we develop it in our children? *Reclaiming Children and Youth, 9*(4), 239–251.

Liepmann, C. M. (1928). Die Selbstventaltung der Gefangenen. In M. Liepmann (Ed.), *Hamburgishe Schriften zur gesamten Strafrechstswessenschaft* (Vol. 12). Mannheim/Berlin/Leipzig.

Loeber, R. (1991). Anti-social behavior: More enduring than changeable? *Journal of American Academy of Child & Adolescent Psychiatry, 30*(3), 393–396.

Loeber, R., & Farrington, D. P. (1998). *Serious and violent juvenile offenders.* Thousand Oaks, CA: Sage.

Long, N. J. (1995). Empowering discipline: Classroom counteraggression. *Journal of Emotional and Behavioral Problems 4*(1), 11–15.

Long, N. J. (2000). Personal struggles in reclaiming troubled students. *Reclaiming Children and Youth, 9*(2), 95–98.

Long, N., Fecser, F., & Brendtro, L. (1998). Life space crisis intervention: New skills for reclaiming students showing patterns of self-defeating behavior. *Healing, 3*(2), 2–22.

Long, N. J., & Morse, W. (1996). *Conflict in the classroom.* Austin, TX: PRO-ED.

Long, N., Wood, M., & Fecser, F. (2001). *Life Space Crisis Intervention.* Austin, TX: PRO-ED.

MacKinnon, R. A., & Michaels, R. (1971). *The psychiatric interview in clinical practice.* Philadelphia: Saunders.

Makarenko, A. (1976). *Anton Makarenko: His life and his work in education.* Moscow, USSR: Progress Press.

Males, M. (1996). *The scapegoat generation: America's war on adolescents.* Monroe, ME: Common Courage Press.

Malone, B. G., Bonitz, D. A., & Rickett, M. M. (1998). Teacher perceptions of disruptive behavior: Maintaining instructional focus. *Educational Horizons, 76,* 189–194.

Marquoit, J., & Dobson, M. (1998). Strength-based treatment for juvenile sexual offenders. *Reclaiming Children and Youth, 7*(1), 40–43.

Maslow, A. (1954). *Motivation and personality.* New York: Harper & Row.

Masterson, J. F. (1981). *The narcissistic and borderline disorders: An integrated developmental approach.* New York: Brunner/Mazel.

Matthews, S. (1995). Juvenile capital offenders on empathy. *Reclaiming Children and Youth, 4*(2), 10–12.

McCarty, B. (1998). "But I have to have a boyfriend!" *Reclaiming Children and Youth, 7*(1), 49–54.

McCluskey, K., & McCluskey, A. (2001). *Understanding ADHD: Our personal journey.* Winnipeg, Manitoba: Portage & Main. (Originally published as *Butterfly Kisses*)

McCord, J. (1990). Problem behaviors. In S. S. Feldman & G. R. Elliot (Eds.), *At the threshold: The developing adolescent* (pp. 414–430). Cambridge, MA: Harvard University Press.

Mead, M. (1979). *Margaret Mead: Some personal views.* London: Angus and Robertson.

Meichenbaum, D., & Fong, G. (1993). How individuals control their own minds: A constructive narrative perspective. In D. M. Wegner & J. W. Pennebaker (Eds.), *Handbook of mental control* (pp. 473–490). Upper Saddle River, NJ: Prentice Hall.

Menninger, K. (1959). Hope. *American Journal of Psychiatry, 116,* 481–491.

Menninger, K. (1963). *The vital balance.* New York: Viking.

Menninger, K. (1988). *The selected correspondence of Karl A. Menninger, 1914–1945.* New Haven, CT: Yale University Press.

Mitchell, M., & McEldowney, J. (2002, June 28). *No disposable kids.* Presentation to the Black Hills Seminars on Reclaiming Youth.

Montessori, M. (1948). *The absorbent mind.* New York: Holt.

Morgan, J. J. P. (1936). *The psychology of the unadjusted school child.* New York: Macmillan.

Morse, W., Cutler, R., & Fink, A. (1964). *Public school classes for the emotionally handicapped: A research analysis.* Reston, VA: Council for Exceptional Children.

Mulvey, E. P., & Cauffman, E. (2001). The inherent limits of predicting school violence. *American Psychologist, 56*(10), 797–802.

Murphy, L. B. (1961). Preventive implications of development in the preschool years. In G. Kaplan (Ed.), *Prevention of mental disorders in children* (pp. 218–248). New York: Basic Books.

Murray, B. (1998). Research reveals potential cause of youthful impulsiveness. *APA Monitor 29*(8), 8.

Nathanson, D. L. (1992). *Shame and pride.* New York: Norton.

NDK. (2003). *Productive peer relationship.* A training curriculum from No Disposable Kids at Starr Commonwealth. Albion, MI: NDK.

Nelson, C. M., Scott, T. M., & Polsgrove, L. (1999). *Perspective on emotional/behavioral disorders: Assumptions and their implications for education and treatment.* Reston, VA: Council for Children with Behavioral Disorders.

Nelson, D. A., & Quick, N. (2002). Parental psychological control: Implications for childhood physical and relational aggression. In B. K. Barber (Ed.), *Intrusive parenting: How psychological control affects children and adolescents* (pp. 161–190). Washington, DC: American Psychological Association.

Nelson, J. R., Roberts, M. L., Mathur, S. R., & Rutherford, R. B., Jr. (1999). Has public policy exceeded our knowledge base? A review of the functional behavioral assessment literature. *Behavioral Disorders, 24,*169–179.

Newman, B., & Newman, P. (1986). *Adolescent development.* Columbus, OH: Merrill.

Nicholls, J. G. (1990). What is ability and why are we mindful of it? A developmental perspective. In R. J. Sternberg & J. Kolligian, Jr. (Eds.), *Competence considered* (pp. 11–40). New Haven, CT: Yale University Press.

Nichols, P. (2000). Bad body fever and deliberate self-injury. *Reclaiming Children and Youth, 9*(3), 151–156.

Nisbett, R. E., & Cohen, D. (1996). *Culture of honor: The psychology of violence in the South.* New York: HarperCollins.

Nolan, E. E., Gadow, K. D., & Sprafkin, J. (2001). Teacher reports of DSM-IV ADHD, ODD, and CD symptoms in schoolchildren. *Journal of the American Academy of Child & Adolescent Psychology, 40*(2), 241–249.

O'Connor, T. G., Rutter, M., & English and Romanian Adoptees Study Team. (2000). Attachment disorder behavior following early severe deprivation: Extension and longitudinal follow-up. *Child and Adolescent Psychiatry, 39*(6), 703–712.

Odney, J., & Brendtro, L. (1992). Students grade their schools. *Journal of Emotional and Behavioral Problems, 2*(1), 4–8.

Olweus, D. (1993). *Bullying at school*. Oxford, UK: Blackwell.

Olweus, D. (1996). Bully/victim problems at school: Facts and effective intervention. *Reclaiming Children and Youth, 5*(1), 15–22.

Osher, D. (2000, July). *Reducing risk and preventing zero tolerance behaviors*. Paper presented at OSEP Research Project Director's Conference, Washington, DC.

Parese, S. (2001, August). *An examination of the frequency of crisis in the lives of troubled students over an academic year*. Paper presented at the Life Space Crisis Intervention Institute, Hagerstown, MD.

Peck, M. S. (1978). *The road less traveled*. New York: Simon & Schuster.

Pennebaker, J. W. (1990). *Opening up*. New York: Avon.

Perry, B., & Pollard, D. (1997). Altered brain development in early childhood. *Society for neuroscience: Proceedings from Annual Meeting*. New Orleans.

Peter, V. (1999a). The idea and the reality of the juvenile court: *Abusus non tollit usus*. *Reclaiming Children and Youth, 8*(3), 134–136.

Peter, V. (1999b). *What makes Boys Town succeed*. Boys Town, NE: Boys Town Press.

Petit, M., & Brooks, T. R. (1998). Abuse and delinquency: Two sides of the same coin. *Reclaiming Children and Youth, 7*(2), 77–79.

Pinker, S. (1997). *How the mind works*. New York: Norton.

Pliszka, S. R., Carlson, C. L., & Swanson, J. M. (1999). *ADHD with comorbid disorders*. New York: Guilford.

Plutchik, R. (1980). *Emotions: A psychoevolutionary synthesis*. New York: Harper & Row.

Polsky, H. (1962). *Cottage six: The social system of delinquent boys in residential treatment*. New York: Russell Sage Foundation.

Pynoos, R. S., Steinberg, A. M., & Wraith, R. (1995). A developmental model of childhood traumatic stress. In D. Cicchetti & D. J. Cohen (Eds.), *Developmental psychopathology: Vol. 2. Risk disorder and adaptation* (pp. 72–95). New York: Wiley.

Quay, H. C., & Hogan, A. E. (1999). *Handbook of disruptive behavior disorders*. New York: Kluwer Academic.

Radke-Yarrow, M., Zahn-Waxler, C., & Chapman, M. (1984). Children's prosocial dispositions and behavior. In P. H. Mussen (Ed.), *Handbook of child psychology: Vol. 4. Socialization, personality, and social development* (pp. 469–545). New York: Wiley.

Rapaport, A. (1960). *Fights, games, and debates.* Ann Arbor: University of Michigan Press.

Raychaba, B. (1990). Empowerment. In F. Kool (Ed.), *The power to change lies within the families.* Rijswijk, Netherlands: Ministry of Welfare, Health and Culture.

Redl, F. (1966). *When we deal with children.* New York: Free Press.

Redl, F. (1994). The oppositional child and the confronting adult: A mind to mind encounter. In E. J. Anthony & D. C. Gilpin (Eds.), *Clinical faces of childhood* (Vol. 1, pp. 41–58). Northvale, NJ: Jason Aronson. (Originally published in 1976)

Redl, F., & Wineman, D. (1951). *Children who hate.* Glencoe, IL: Free Press.

Redl, F., & Wineman, D. (1952). *Controls from within: Techniques for the treatment of the aggressive child.* Glencoe, IL: Free Press.

Redl, F., & Wineman, D. (1957). *The aggressive child.* Glencoe, IL: Free Press.

Reid, J., Patterson, G. R., & Snyder, J. (Eds.). (2002). *Antisocial behavior in children and adolescents.* Washington, DC: American Psychological Association.

Rhodes, W., & Hoey, K. (1994). *Overcoming childhood misfortune: Children who beat the odds.* Westport, CT: Praeger.

Richards, P. S., & Bergin, A. E. (1997). *A spiritual strategy for counseling and psychotherapy.* Washington, DC: American Psychological Association.

Roberts, M. (2001). *Horse sense for people.* New York: Viking.

Roberts, S., & Jurren, A. (1968). *Life space interview. Workshop in learning and behavior.* U.S. Office of Education. University of Michigan, Ann Arbor.

Rogers, C. (1939). *The clinical treatment of the problem child.* Boston: Houghton Mifflin.

Rogoff, B., & Morelli, G. (1989). Perspectives on children's development from cultural psychology. *American Psychologist, 44*(2), 343–348.

Ross, C. A. (2000). *The trauma model.* Richardson, TX: Manitou Communications.

Rothbaum, F., & Weisz, J. R. (1989). *Child psychopathology and the quest for control.* Newbury Park, CA: Sage.

Rudolph, S. M., & Epstein, M. H. (2000). Empowering children and families through strength-based assessment. *Reclaiming Children and Youth, 8*(4), 207–209.

Rutstein, N. (2000). Frontiers in healing racism. *Reclaiming Children and Youth, 9*(1), 29–35.

Safran, J. D., Crocker, P., McMain, S., & Murray, P. (1990). Therapeutic alliance rupture as a therapy event for empirical investigation. *Psychotherapy: Theory, Research, and Practice, 27,* 159–165.

Safran, J. D., & Muran, J. C. (2000). *Negotiating the therapeutic alliance: A relational treatment guide.* New York: Guilford.

Sagi, A., & Hoffman, M. L. (1976). Empathic distress in the newborn. *Developmental Psychopathology, 12,* 175–176.

Salovey, P., Bedell, B. T., Detweiler, J. B., & Mayer, J. D. (2000). Current directions in emotional intelligence research. In M. Lewis & J. Haviland-Jones (Eds.), *Handbook of emotions* (2nd ed., pp. 504–520). New York: Guilford.

Salovey, P., Hsee, C. K., & Mayer, J. D. (1993). Emotional intelligence and the self-regulation of affect. In D. M. Wegner & J. W. Pennebaker (Eds.), *Handbook of mental control* (pp. 258–277). Upper Saddle River, NJ: Prentice Hall.

Sameroff, A. J. (2000). Dialectical processes in developmental psychopathology. In A. J. Sameroff, M. Lewis, & S. Miller (Eds.), *Handbook of Developmental Psychopathology* (2nd ed., pp. 23–40). New York: Plenum.

Sanders, W. B. (1970). *Juvenile offenders for a thousand years.* Chapel Hill: University of North Carolina Press.

Sapolsky, B. S., Stocking, S. H., & Zillman, D. (1977). Immediate versus delayed retaliation in male and female adults. *Psychological Reports, 40,* 197–198.

Schoenwald, S., Borduin, C., & Henggeler, S. (1998). Multisystemic therapy: Changing the natural and service ecologies of adolescents and families. In M. H. Epstein, K. Kutash, & A. Duchnowski (Eds.), *Outcomes for children & youth with behavioral and emotional disorders and their families: Programs and evaluation best practices* (pp. 485–512). Austin, TX: PRO-ED.

Scotti, J., Morris, T., McNeil, C., & Hawkins, R. (1996). DSM-IV and disorders of childhood and adolescence. Can structural criteria be functional? *Journal of Consulting and Clinical Psychology, 64,* 1177–1191.

Seita, J., & Brendtro, L. (2002). *Kids who outwit adults.* Longmont, CO: Sopris West.

Seita, J., Mitchell, M., & Tobin, C. (1996). *In whose best interest?* Elizabethtown, PA: Continental Press.

Seligman, M., & Csikszentmihalyi, M. (2000). Positive psychology: An introduction. *American Psychologist, 55*(1), 5–14.

Selye, H. (1978). *The stress of life* (Rev. ed.). New York: McGraw-Hill.

Shantz, C. U., & Hartup, W. W. (Eds.). (1992). *Conflict in child and adolescent development.* New York: Cambridge University Press.

Sherman, L. W. (1993). Defiance, deterrence, and irrelevance: A theory of the criminal sanction. *Journal of Research in Crime and Delinquency, 30*(4), 445–477.

Shores, R. E., Gunter, P. L., & Jack, S. L. (1993). Classroom management strategies: Are they setting events for coercion? *Behavioral Disorders, 18,* 92–102.

Skinner, B. F. (1953). *Science and human behavior.* New York: Macmillan.

Snyder, J. (2002). Reinforcement and coercion mechanisms in the development of antisocial behavior: Peer relationships. In J. B. Reid, G. R. Patterson, & J. Snyder (Eds.), *Antisocial behavior in children and adolescents* (pp. 101–122). Washington, DC: American Psychological Association.

Spence, D. (1984). *Narrative truth and historical truth.* New York: Norton.

Sroufe, L. A. (1990). Considering the normal and abnormal together: The essence of developmental psychopathology. *Development and Psychopathology, 2,* 235–247.

Stanley, P. H., & Purkey, W. W. (1994). Student self-concept-as-learner: Does invitational education make a difference? *Research in the Schools, 1*(2), 15–22.

Stone, G., Buehler, C., & Barber, B. K. (2002). Interparental conflict, parental psychological control, and youth problem behavior. In B. K. Barber (Ed.), *Intrusive parenting* (pp. 53–96). Washington, DC: American Psychological Association.

Stott, D. (1982). *Delinquency: The problem and its prevention.* New York: Spectrum.

Strommen, M. (1988). *Five cries of youth.* San Francisco: Harper & Row.

Sugai, G., & Lewis, T. J. (1999). *Developing positive behavioral support for students with challenging behaviors.* Reston, VA: Council for Children with Behavioral Disorders.

Sullivan, H. S. (1953). *The interpersonal theory of psychiatry.* New York: Norton.

Taylor, J. McLean, Gilligan, C., & Sullivan, A. M. (1996). "What gets me into trouble is my big mouth!!" Women and girls, race and relationship. *Reclaiming Children and Youth, 5*(2), 68–73.

Terry, W. (1997). Parents confront the NIMBY hysteria. *Reclaiming Children and Youth, 6*(3), 144–146.

Thomas, A., & Chess, S. (1977). *Temperament and development.* New York: Brunner/Mazel.

Thousand, J. S., & Villa, R. A. (Eds.). (2000). *Restructuring for caring and effective education: Piecing the puzzle together* (2nd ed.). Baltimore: Paul H. Brookes.

Tompkins, S. S. (1963). *Affect/Imagery/Consciousness: Vols. 1–2.* New York: Springer.

Torrance, E. P. (1965). *Constructive behavior: Stress, personality, and mental health.* Belmont, CA: Wadsworth.

Trieschman, A. E., Whittaker, J. K., & Brendtro, L. K. (1969). *The other 23 hours.* New York: Aldine de Gruyter.

Trulson, C., Triplett, R., & Snell, C. (2001). Social control in a school setting: Evaluating a school-based boot camp. *Crime and Delinquency, 47*(4), 573–609.

Van Bockern, S. (2000). Personal communication.

Vanderven, K. (2000). Cultural aspects of point and level systems. *Reclaiming Children and Youth, 9*(1), 53–59.

Van Doren, C. (1991). *A history of knowledge.* New York: Ballantine Books.

Vilakazi, H. (1993). Rediscovering lost truths. *Journal of Emotional and Behavioral Problems, 1*(4), 37.

Vorrath, H., & Brendtro, L. (1985). *Positive Peer Culture* (2nd ed.). New York: Aldine de Gruyter.

Vossekuil, B., Reddy, M., Fine, R., Borum, R., & Modzeleski, W. (2000). *USSS Safe School Initiative: An interim report on the prevention of targeted violence in schools.* Washington, DC: U.S. Secret Service National Threat Assessment Center.

Vygotsky, L. (1962). *Thought and language.* Cambridge, MA: MIT Press.

Warger, C. L., & Rutherford, R. B., Jr. (1996). *A collaborative approach to teaching social skills.* Reston, VA: Foundation for Exceptional Innovations.

Webster, R. A. (2002). Symptoms and long-term outcomes for children who have been sexually assaulted. *Psychology in the Schools, 38*(6), 533–549.

Webster-Stratton, C., & Herbert, M. (1994). *Troubled families, problem children.* New York: Wiley.

Werner, E., Bierman, J., & French, F. (1971). *Children of Kauai: A longitudinal study from the prenatal period to age ten.* Honolulu: University of Hawaii Press.

Werner, E., & Smith, R. (1992). *Overcoming the odds: High risk children from birth to adulthood.* Ithaca, NY: Cornell University Press.

White, R. W. (1959). Motivation reconsidered: The concept of competence. *Psychological Review, 66,* 297–333.

Wilker, K. (1920). *Der Lindenhof.* (English translation by Stephan Lhotzky, 1993.) Sioux Falls, SD: Augustana College.

Winnicott, D. W. (1965). *The maturational processes and the facilitating environment: Studies in the theory of emotional development.* New York: International Universities Press.

Wolff, T. (1989). *This boy's life: A memoir.* New York: Atlantic Monthly Press.

Wood, F. H. (1988, Summer). Factors in intervention choice [Monograph]. *Behavioral Disorders, 11,* 133–143.

Wood, F. H. (1995). Positive responses to student resistance to programs of behavior change. *Reclaiming Children and Youth, 4*(1), 30–33.

Wood, M. (2000). Cited in S. Larson & L. Brendtro, *Reclaiming our prodigal sons and daughters.* Bloomington, IN: National Educational Service.

Zeigarnik, B. (1926). Das Behalten von erledigten und unerledigten Handlungen (The memory of completed and uncompleted tasks). *Psychologische Forschung, 9,* 1–85.

Zillman, D. (1993). Mental control of angry aggression. In D. M. Wegner & J. W. Pennebaker (Eds.), *Handbook of mental control* (pp. 370–392). Upper Saddle River, NJ: Prentice-Hall.

Zillman, D., & Cantor, J. R. (1976). Effective timing of information about mitigating circumstances on emotional responses to provocation and retaliatory behavior. *Journal of Experimental Social Psychology, 12,* 38–55.

Index

Note. Figures, tables, and notes are represented by the italicized letters *f, t,* and *n* following the page number.

About the Authors

Larry Brendtro is president of Reclaiming Youth and past president of Starr Commonwealth, serving troubled youth in Michigan and Ohio. He currently serves as dean of Starr's International Research Council. He has been a youth worker, teacher, principal, and psychologist. He started the graduate program in children's behavior disorders at the University of Illinois and taught at The Ohio State University and Augustana College. He has authored 10 books related to troubled children and has trained professionals worldwide. He and Nicholas Long founded the journal *Reclaiming Children and Youth*. He holds a Ph.D. from the University of Michigan in the combined program in education and psychology.

Reclaiming Youth is a nonprofit education and research organization working on behalf of children in conflict within the home, the school, and the community. With offices in South Dakota and Michigan, Reclaiming Youth provides strength-based training at the Black Hills Seminars and at professional development conferences in North America and abroad. The Reclaiming Youth mission is grounded in the Circle of Courage, which portrays four universal needs for positive growth: belonging, mastery, independence, and generosity. For information about the Reclaiming Youth network, contact Reclaiming Youth, P.O. Box 57, Lennox, SD 57039, **www.reclaiming.com**.

Mary Shahbazian is president of the Allendale Association, which operates educational and treatment programs at various sites in Illinois and Wisconsin. She has 25 years of experience in developing programs for troubled children and their families, serving in roles as child and youth care worker, group counselor, special educator, principal, and agency executive. She is a national senior trainer in Life Space Crisis Intervention and an advisor to numerous private and public bodies concerned with children at risk. She holds graduate degrees in special education and social service administration, and recently completed a master's degree in jurisprudence in child and family law at Loyola University.

Allendale was founded over 100 years ago as a private, non-profit charity for needy children and families. Allendale offers a range of alternative schools, residential treatment, foster care, transitional living programs, and child and family counseling programs at sites in Illinois and Wisconsin. The Allendale philosophy is a strength-based approach to children and adolescents who exhibit emotional and behavioral disabilities. Allendale is a national training site for professionals in the fields of psychology, special education, and child and youth care. For information, contact Allendale Association, P.O. Box 1088, Lake Villa, IL 60046, **www.allendale4kids.org**.